# JERUSALEM
## CITY OF
## THE GREAT KING

STORK TOWER
Suleiman
Derekh Yeriho
SHA'AR HA-PERAHIM (HEROD'S GATE)
JEREMIAH'S GROTTO
Derekh Shekhem
FRANCISCAN SISTERS CONVENT
SHA'AR SHEKHEM (DAMASCUS GATE)
DOME OF THE ROCK (MOSQUE OF OMAR)
KIPPAT HA-SELA
EL AQSA MOSQUE
SOLOMON'S STABLES
HA-KOTEL HA-MA'ARAVI (WAILING WALL)
FRENCH HOSPITAL
CHURCH OF THE REDEEMER
Mamillah
SHA'AR YAFO (JAFFA GATE)
THE CITADEL
Derekh Hevron
SHA'AR HA-ASHPOT (DUNG GATE)
CHURCH OF THE DORMITION

Volume Two

# Jerusalem
## City of the Great King

R. Steven Notley

cartaJerusalem

First published in 2015 by
**CARTA Jerusalem**


11 Rivka Street, P.O.B. 2500
Jerusalem 9102401, Israel
E-mail: carta@carta.co.il
www.carta-jerusalem.com

Cartography: Carta Jerusalem
Cover photograph: Shmuel Magal
The southern steps leading to the Temple Mount
Frontispiece: Map of Jerusalem by Hermann Bollmann, 1970

Great care has been taken to cite all sources of illustrations whenever known. If inadvertently we failed to do so, due credit will be given in the following edition.



ISBN: 978-965-220-866-8

Printed in Israel

# Contents

*For Sunya*

# PREFACE

The ancient Greeks tell the story of King Sisyphus, who was punished by Zeus because of the mortal's hubris (Homer *Od.* 11.13). For his punishment the king was forced to roll an immense boulder up a hill. However, the stone was enchanted and always rolled away from Sisyphus before reaching the top. The boulder returned to the bottom of the hill, thus assuring the king a never-ending task. The legend lent its name to the eponymous challenge of *sisyphean* (unending) tasks.

Anyone who has thought to write on the archaeology of Jerusalem knows well that it likewise is a *sisyphean* task. Archaeology in Jerusalem is barely over a century old and continues to unfold before our eyes. Particularly the last fifty years have seen significantly increased efforts to discover the city's past. New finds every year render what is previously written almost out of date before the ink is dry. With an acknowledgement of this reality, together with a recognition that much of the Old City of Jerusalem remains inaccessible to archaeological investigation, the present work lays its shoulder to the challenge.

In previous centuries, locals, pilgrims, and explorers observed primarily the visible vestiges of the city's history lying on the surface. Sometimes they even braved the risks to enter the city's bowels—its cisterns and subterranean channels. Captain Charles Warren famously dug 27 shafts to investigate what lay hidden beneath Jerusalem's surface. Danger lurked at every moment because of the mountains of debris through which they tunneled, which could shift and sometimes did collapse. Warren's efforts were published in a book aptly named, *Underground Jerusalem* (1876). His underground exploration, particularly in the vicinity of the Haram esh-Sharif (the Noble Sanctuary), site of Solomon and Herod's temples, was necessitated by the local sensitivities about archaeological work around the Muslim shrine.

Warren is not the only person who has triggered Muslim concerns about Jerusalem archaeology. A remarkable tale is told of a British aristocrat, Montague Brownlow Parker, 5th Earl of Morley, who organized excavations in 1909 and 1911 in the Ophel in search of the legendary treasures of Solomon's Temple. Frustrated over the meager results, he bribed the governor of Jerusalem to allow his party to investigate the Temple Mount. For $25,000 the hereditary guardian of the mosque turned a blind eye as Parker and his accomplices entered under the cloak of darkness, dressed in Arab garb. They first explored the subterranean space below the esplanade known as Solomon's Stables, but then shifted their attention to the Dome of the Rock and the natural cavern beneath the surface of the sacred rock, which Muslims believe bears the footprint of Mohammed's steed that bore him on his heavenly journey. In an unfortunate twist of fate, an uninformed attendant decided to stay overnight in the shrine. Hearing the clamor of Parker's excavation, he came upon the ongoing work and what he considered desecration of the sacred site. He rushed out, informed the authorities, and soon the news filled Jerusalem. Chaos ensued. The misbegotten venture left behind riots and disturbances in Jerusalem, while Parker and his men fled to Jaffa where they escaped by ship safely back to England. Knowing something of the early history of archaeology in Jerusalem, the lingering suspicions that exist even in our own day come as little surprise.

The reunification of Jerusalem in 1967 brought the beginning of Israeli archeological work in the Old City of Jerusalem. The opportunity to investigate the largely unoccupied Jewish Quarter fell to Nahman Avigad of the Hebrew University from 1969 to 1982. The results have been published posthumously (2004–2014) by his student Hillel Geva. Work immediately south and west of the Temple Mount, an area in biblical times known as the Ophel, was undertaken by Benjamin Mazar from 1968 to 1977. In more recent years, his granddaughter Eilat Mazar has led excavations in the upper portions of the City of David, where she claims to have unearthed the monumental walls of the stronghold of Zion (2 Sam 5:7). Areas of the City of David have been the object of extensive excavations by numerous scholars since the days of Warren. Notable in recent years is the work of Eli Shukron and Ronny Reich, who have provided us with a better understanding of Canaanite and early

Israelite settlement in Jerusalem, especially the city's water installations.

The work of many others who have excavated in Jerusalem could be cited, but there simply is not enough space to mention them here. Nevertheless, one additional note must be included about a valuable work being carried out as a result of unfortunate circumstances. In 1996 the Muslim authorities (the Waqf) responsible for the Haram began construction in Solomon's Stables and the eastern Huldah Gate. They built a subterranean prayer space called the Marwani Musalla, which can accommodate 7,000 individuals. In 1997, the Western Huldah Gate passageway was converted into yet another mosque.

To build these the Waqf had to demolish and remove existing structures and artifacts that had been in place for millennia. This treasure of archaeological and historical information was vacated without scientific examination, loaded into dump trucks and discarded on the nearby slopes of the Mount of Olives. Whatever one's political or religious persuasion, the willful destruction of archaeoloigcal remains from a site protected as a UN World Heritage Site should warrant unqualified condemnation.

Under less than ideal circumstances, Gabriel Barkay and Zachi Dvira have taken on the task to sift and examine the debris deposited on the Mount of Olives. While the remains are no longer *in situ*, there is no question about their place of origin. These items may still provide some fragmentary insight into the history of the Temple Mount. For example, the discovery of first-century opus sectile tiles aids us to reconstruct the Herodian pavement that adorned the temple precincts, its stylistic connection to the Roman-styled opus sectile tiles in Herod's winter palace at Jericho, and perhaps the meaning of the Greek term *lithostratos* in John 19:13 that describes the pavement in Herod's Royal Palace in the upper city of Jerusalem. Josephus uses the Greek term twice (*J.W.* 6:85–86; 6:189), and in both instances it is in reference to the Herodian opus sectile pavement of the temple precincts.

To bring together this mosaic of evidence, the investigator must be familiar with the results of recent archaeological investigations and understand them in light of a careful reading of the ancient literary witnesses (biblical and extra-biblical). Attention must be given to the nuances of language that inform us in the Greek and Hebrew literature. This is no simple task, and it falls precisely at the juncture of history, philology, and archaeology. To deny the voice of one discipline over the others can leave us short of a clear understanding of history and its topographical details.

My own training falls more within the field of historical philology and historical inquiry. I was privileged to study with David Flusser at the Hebrew University. My research interest is in Jewish literature and thought of the Second Temple period and its importance for our understanding of Jesus and the origins of Christianity. Much of my work has come through a critical engagement with literary works originating in Greco-Roman antiquity. While still a student I was invited by the Anglican Church to initiate and develop a study program with field trips for Christians visiting the Holy Land. It was this experience that brought my attention to the value of reading history in the context of its physical setting. It was my introduction to the integrated multi-disciplinary approach of historical geography: history, topography, philology, and archaeology. It also prepared me for my later work with Anson F. Rainey and our publication of *The Sacred Bridge: Carta's Atlas of the Biblical World* (2006, 2014). For sixteen years I had the opportunity to live, study, and teach in Jerusalem. My reading of history (biblical and extra-biblical) was illumined by the discovery of the physical contours of the historical narrative.

During those years, Jerusalem was home. Two of our four children were born in Jerusalem, and though since relocated to the U.S. some still indicate Jerusalem as home on their Facebook pages. Since I returned to the U.S. in 2001 to teach at Nyack College in New York City, I have had the chance to return to Israel several times each year. It has allowed me to keep abreast of the fast-paced, changing scene of advances in Jerusalem and Israel archaeology. I have continued collaborative research and publication with Israeli scholars. My own understanding continues to be deepened because of this rich scholarly interaction.

To a large extent the present work is the fruit of thirty years of engagement with the land and scholarship in Israel. I have had the chance to explore the landscape of Jerusalem and its environs—from Dan to Beersheba. I am indebted to those with whom I have studied formally and informally, both to my teachers and to my students; and to those students, friends and family who have joined me in my travels.

In the writing of this book I have been especially helped by the insights and comments of Hillel Geva and Marc Turnage. Their willingness to read the manuscript and offer suggestions is much appreciated. Once again, Emanuel and Shay Hausman of Carta Jerusalem have been a constant source of encouragement and wisdom. Barbara Ball has risen to the challenge once more, to bring her considerable gifts and talent to improve upon my ramblings.

Yet, of all those to whom I am most indebted for both the richness of this journey and the resulting content of this book, there is one without whose understanding and encouragement this work would never have seen the light of day. In January 1983, I returned from a month in Jerusalem and informed my wife, Sunya, that I wanted to try my hand at Ph.D. studies at the Hebrew University. We packed up our things, tied up ends and on March 13, 1983, we traveled with our two young children, embarking on an adventure that continues. Throughout those sixteen years, not always easy ones, including the 1991 Gulf War and two *intifadas*, she remained a source of strength and a full partner in this journey. Without her presence alongside me, none of what appears within the covers of this book would have been possible. No words can adequately express my love and gratitude for our life together, richly lived. It is with a heart full of thanks that I dedicate this book to Sunya.

**R. Steven Notley, Ph.D.**
Nyack College
New York City

## THE TOPOGRAPHY OF JERUSALEM

CHAPTER 1

# Pre-Herodian History

The capital city of Judea in the first century A.D. barely resembled its humble beginnings in the days of King David. The Israelite monarch who was crowned king in Hebron (2 Sam 2:4), the tribal center of Judah, realized that he needed a capital more geographically central. The choice of the Jebusite city was no accident. The centrifugal political forces that played out in the tribal confederation had long challenged centralized authority. David's new city was more geographically central than the historic and important city of Hebron. Lying on the border between Judah and Benjamin—but not yet included in conquered land—it retained a measure of independence from individual tribal control. It also lay near the lines of economic travel in the hill country. It was close (yet securely secluded) from the watershed route, the ancient Way of the Patriarchs (Judg 21:19; Bethel, Shechem, Bethlehem, Hebron). North of Jerusalem was the important east-west crossroad, which provided western access to the hill country and Jerusalem from the coast along the ascent of Beth-horon (Josh 10:10; 1 Macc 3:16). After intersecting the plateau in the tribal allotment of Benjamin, the route descended into the Judean Wilderness, to the fords of the Jordan River and ascended again to the Transjordanian highlands (cf. 1 Sam 13:18).

Yet as vital as the geographical, political and economic dimensions of David's new capital were, the most important development was the transformation of Jerusalem into the cultic center of the kingdom. The building of the temple in Jerusalem consolidated Jerusalem's identity as the epicenter of the nation. Even in the subsequent centuries when the kingdom was divided, the attraction of Jerusalem's temple continued (1 Kgs 12:26–27). The final stage in the development of Jerusalem's spiritual importance is attested in 2 Chronicles—one of the latest works of the Hebrew Scriptures—in which Jerusalem's Temple Mount is identified with Moriah—the place of Abraham's offering of Isaac (cf. 2 Chr 3:1; Jub. 18:13; *Ant.* 1:223–226). This identification of the mount finds no mention in the biblical account of the binding of Isaac, the place of which is called instead the *region of Moriah* (Gen 22:2), or the early descriptions of David's purchase of the threshing floor from Araunah the Jebusite, on which later the temple stood (2 Sam 24:18–25).

The topography of Jerusalem shaped its development. Jerusalem of the first century A.D. spread over four hills with an intervening central valley, but the earliest settlement by the Jebusites was limited to the lower spur of the eastern hill. The location was strategic. All three requirements of ancient settlement can be identified with the site of Canaanite Jerusalem: trade, security, and water. As the story from Judges accurately describes, the Jebusite city was near the ancient watershed route from Bethlehem to Gibeah (Judg 19:11–12). It was protected on the west by the lower portions of the central valley and on the east by the Kidron Valley. These two ravines joined the Hinnom Valley south of the ancient city, providing a formidable natural defense from the east, south and west. There are also hints of an earlier transversal vale between the northern edge of the Jebusite city and the upper portions of the eastern hill where the temple later stood (see Millo: 2 Sam 5:9; 1 Kgs 11:27). As for water, recent archaeological discoveries have illuminated the effort by the early Canaanite residents to gain and protect access to the waters of the Gihon Spring.

This then was the Jebusite "stronghold of Zion" that David conquered and renamed the City of David (2 Sam 5:7; 1 Chr 11:5). It is a twist of historical irony that the Canaanite *ṣîôn*, the pre-Davidic, Jebusite

**JERUSALEM AT THE TIME OF HEZEKIAH 701 B.C.**

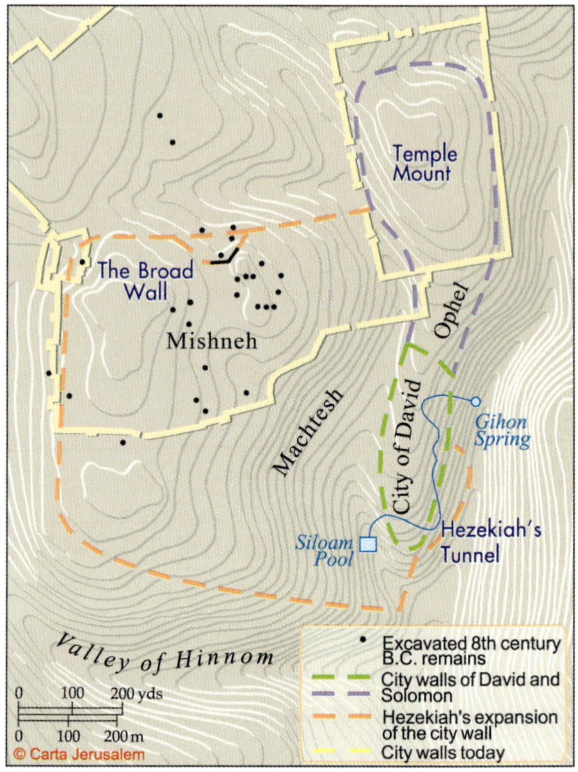

*View of the stepped stone structure in Area G in the City of David.* (photo Ricardo Tulio Gandelman from Rio de Janeiro, Brazil, via Wikimedia Commons)

name for Jerusalem, has become so linked to the Jewish identification with the city for three millennia. Throughout Jerusalem's history it has expanded and contracted, often mirroring political developments in the nation at large. Times of peace, stability, growth and independence resulted in expansion of the city. In the days of the First Temple, Jerusalem reached its largest expanse during the reign of Hezekiah (716–687 B.C.). He was the first to extend the defensive walls of Jerusalem to encompass the western hill.

*Remains of the Broad Wall in the Jewish Quarter of the Old City; the scale on the house shows the former height of the wall.* (photo TijsB from the Hague, Netherlands, via Wikimedia Commons)

A few years prior (722 B.C.), Sargon II had conquered the northern kingdom of Israel. Typically, the walled cities were the residence of a nation's elite: royalty, military and important administrative figures in the kingdom. Hezekiah took the unusual step of building a substantial wall to encircle the western hill and to protect the extramural population. The unparalleled scale of what Nahman Avigad called Hezekiah's "broad wall" demonstrates the concern the king had for Jerusalem's defenses from the north. The prophet Isaiah commended Hezekiah for his initiative, but also criticized him for destroying homes in the construction of the wall (Isa 22:10). Modern excavations uncovered evidence both of Hezekiah's defensive wall and the houses that were destroyed to build it.

Of course, Hezekiah's actions were not altruistic. He sought to defend the city from the looming threat posed by Sargon's successor, Sennacherib. According to the biblical accounts, the city withstood the Assyrian's siege in 701 B.C. Hezekiah's successful defense may be indicated by the omission of Jerusalem from the Assyrian relief panels chronicling Sennacherib's conquests in Judah. The wording of Sennacherib's prism that he shut up Hezekiah "like a caged bird," fails to make mention of his conquest of the capital. Still, a little over a century later, Jerusalem was conquered by another kingdom from the east, the Babylonians led by Nebuchadnezzar in 597 B.C. Both Jerusalem and the temple built by Solomon were leveled after an eighteen-month siege in 586 B.C. Over the next century the city remained mostly rubble and sparsely populated (2 Kgs 25:8–12).

When Cyrus and the Persians conquered the kingdom of Babylonia in 539 B.C. they repatriated foreign captives—including the Judeans—to their homelands. The territory of Judah became a Persian province called Yehud. Persian policy was one of religious tolerance with priests and administrative appointments often carrying out self-administration. Over the protests of the Samaritans, the Persians allowed the walls of Jerusalem to be rebuilt (Ezra 1:2–3). However, these efforts

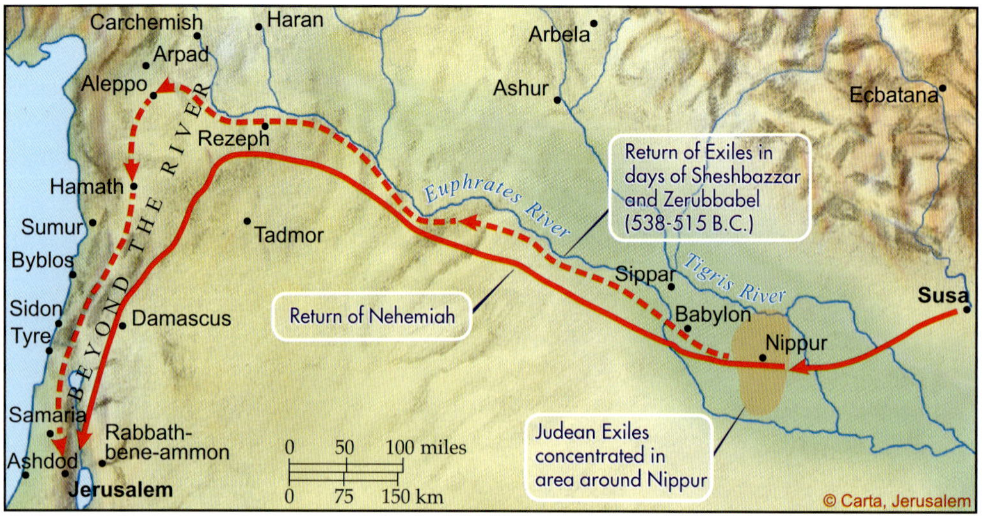


## THE RETURN FROM EXILE

were limited to the eastern hill. In 520 B.C. renewed efforts led by a Davidic descendant, Zerubbabel son of Shealtiel, and the priest Joshua son of Jehozadak began to rebuild the temple. Once again they met resistance, and it was not until Cyrus' original edict was rediscovered in 515 B.C. that the initiative was completed.

Ezra the Scribe returned to Jerusalem in 458 B.C. and is credited with consolidating the religious community around legal matters. His failed attempts to fortify Jerusalem further (cf. Ezra 4:7–16) were followed by those of the new governor Nehemiah who arrived in 445 B.C. The latter initiated the first priority to rebuild the walls of Jerusalem (Neh 1–2), and he organized the people to complete the task in 52 days. The Book of Nehemiah presents the most detailed description of Jerusalem in the Persian period, which seems only to have included the eastern hill with walls that enclosed the temple and the City of David. It also mentions the Birah, a fortress that stood near the temple and which Nehemiah used as his headquarters (Neh 2:8; 7:2). Not only is Nehemiah credited with the refortification of the capital, he also strengthened the efforts to repopulate the city. In his decrees, he compelled parts of the population to reside in the city. The picture we receive in the time of Nehemiah remains until the coming of the Hellenistic conquerors.

## JERUSALEM AT THE TIME OF NEHEMIAH

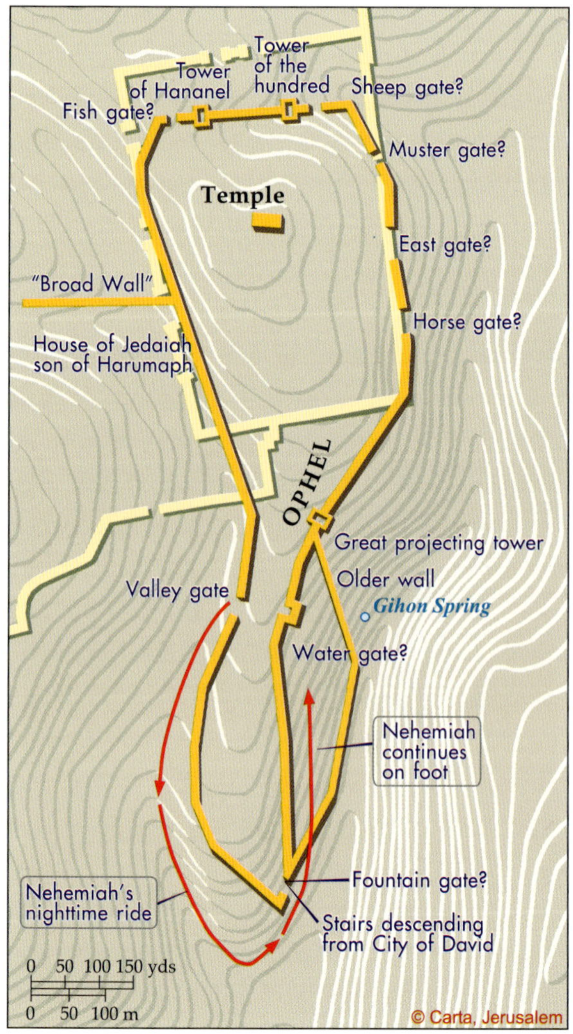

CHAPTER 2

# Jerusalem in the Early Hellenistic Period

Persian domination of the Near East came to an abrupt end with the remarkable campaign of Alexander, son of Philip king of Macedonia. His conquest of Anatolia, the Levant, Egypt, Mesopotamia and the land of Persia up to the borders of India earned him the title, Alexander the Great. Following the defeat of the Persian Darius at Issus in 333 B.C., Alexander marched down the Mediterranean coast towards his primary objective to the south: Egypt. In spite of the various legends concerning Alexander and the interior of Judea, his priorities were clearly elsewhere.

On the march through Phoenicia to Egypt his only pauses were the sieges of Tyre and Gaza. Josephus reports that the Samaritan Sanballat approached Alexander at Tyre offering his fealty and material support. Certainly the Macedonian would have requested and expected local sapatries to transfer their allegiances to the new sovereign. It is also not unimaginable that there was contact between the leadership in Jerusalem and Alexander (cf. *Ant.* 11:329). Where and when Alexander encountered the Jewish hierarchy from Jerusalem during his conquest of the region remains uncertain. Nevertheless, when he arrived in the east, he had with him Jewish conscripts.

Alexander's sudden death in 323 B.C. resulted in the necessary distribution of powers among his subordinates. Although his tenure was short, the Macedonian's introduction of Hellenism to the Near East had lasting consequences for Jerusalem and Judea. Over the next century and a half, Jerusalem would find itself caught between the regional aspirations of Alexander's successors. First transpired the period of the Diadochi (the "successors") with changes in political control of the Syrian lands five times—320, 315, 312, 302 and 301 B.C. This was followed by the whole of the third century, which was marked by a struggle called the four "Syrian Wars," during which the Ptolemaic kingdom in Egypt vied with the Seleucid kingdom in Syria, often with Judea in the crosshairs of the conflict.

Not only did Hellenistic domination of the region bring political consequences in the Near East, it influenced internal politics, material culture and introduced the Greek language. A century later the Jewish community in Alexandria, Egypt, translated the Hebrew Bible for the first time into a local non-Hebrew vernacular—the Greek Bible (Septuagint).

Yet, the new foreign customs often were at odds with ancient traditions, and the limits of accommodation to the foreign culture became the point of conflict between hierocratic factions in Jerusalem—the Tobiads and Oniads. Each competed with the other to enlist the support of ever changing Seleucid rulers, sometimes to the compromise of ancestral taboos. With the advent of Antiochus IV Epiphanes things reached a breaking point.

> [Antiochus] authorized [the population of Judea] to observe the ordinances of the Gentiles. So they built a gymnasium in Jerusalem, according to Gentile custom, and removed the marks of circumcision, and abandoned the holy covenant. They joined with the Gentiles and sold themselves to do evil. (1 Macc 1:12b–15)

> The priests were no longer intent upon their service at the altar. Despising the sanctuary and neglecting the sacrifices, they hurried to take part in the unlawful proceedings in the wrestling arena after the signal for the discus-throwing, disdaining the honors prized by their ancestors and putting the highest value upon Greek forms of prestige. (2 Macc 4:14–15)

The reason for Antiochus' imposition of Greek customs on the Jewish population is the subject of scholarly debate. He had assumed the throne after the brief reign of his brother Seleucus IV Philopater in 175 B.C. (Polyb. 26; Livy 41.20; Diod. Sic. 29.32; 31.16). Both inherited a weakened empire from their father, Antiochus III the Great. The Romans had defeated Antiochus III at Magnesia ad Sipylum in 190 B.C., and the Treaty of Apamea required him to pay severe war reparations. These financial burdens and the curtailing of political adventurism were passed along to Seleucus and Antiochus Epiphanes, and likely contributed to unfortunate missteps with the Jewish population in Judea.

Antiochus Epiphanes sought to expand his kingdom to include Ptolemaic Egypt. After an unsuccessful campaign that ended at Alexandria in 170/169 B.C., he withdrew to Syria. Upon his retreat, he visited Jerusalem in need of funds. "Antiochus dared to enter the most holy temple in all the

**EGYPTIAN CAMPAIGNS OF ANTIOCHUS IV 170–167 B.C.**

world, guided by [the high priest] Menelaus, who had become a traitor both to the laws and to his country" (2 Macc 5:15).

> The raid of Antiochus [Epiphanes] on the temple was iniquitous, that it was impecuniosity which drove him to invade it, when he was not an open enemy, that he attacked us, his allies and friends, and that he found there nothing to deserve ridicule. (*Apion* 2:83)

*Tetradrachma of Antiochus IV Epiphanes.*

During a second Seleucid campaign into Egypt in the following year, at Eleusis on the outskirts of Alexandria, the Roman Senate ordered Antiochus to withdraw and to return to his own lands (Polyb. 29.27; Diod. Sic. 31.2; Livy 45.12; App. *Syr.* 66; Justin. *Epit.* 34.3). His failure to conquer Egypt spawned false rumors that he had been killed in the Egyptian campaign. Chaos and disturbances broke out in Judea. Antiochus assumed the country was in open rebellion. He could hardly allow his reversals in Egypt to give the impression of weakness to his subjects.

> So, raging inwardly, he left Egypt and took [Jerusalem] by storm. And he commanded his soldiers to cut down relentlessly every one they met and to slay those who went into the houses. Then there was killing of young and old, destruction of boys, women, and children, and slaughter of virgins and infants. Within the total of three days eighty thousand were destroyed, forty thousand in hand-to-hand fighting; and as many were sold into slavery as were slain. (2 Macc 5:11–14)

The author of First Maccabees only remarks that "[Antiochus] went up against Israel and came to Jerusalem with a strong force" (1 Macc 1:20). Like other ancient historians, Jason the Cyrene, whose literary work is the source for Second Maccabees, has exaggerated the slaughter in Jerusalem, though there is little reason to question that Antiochus responded to the uprising there with force. Both reports recount with outrage the king's desecration of the temple when he entered it.

> He took the holy vessels with his polluted hands, and swept away with profane hands the votive offerings which other kings had made to enhance the glory and honor of the place.…So Antiochus carried off eighteen hundred talents from the temple and hurried away to Antioch, thinking in his arrogance that he could sail on the land and walk on the sea, because his mind was elated. (1 Macc 1:21–23; 2 Macc 5:16, 21)

The king now took steps to assure that rebellion would not take hold in Judea. He sent Apollonius, captain of the Mysians, with a considerable force (1 Macc 1:29–30; 2 Macc 5:24). Apollonius sought to assure the continued loyalty of the people to the Seleucid ruler. First Maccabees records that at this time, "they fortified the city of David with a strong wall and strong towers, and it became their *citadel*" (i.e., Gk: Akra; 1 Macc 1:33). In addition, Antiochus stationed a garrison of foreign troops within the fortifications (1 Macc 1:34–38). These two initiatives by Apollonius on the orders of the Seleucid king would prove to be irritants to the people of Jerusalem for decades.

Reaction from the local citizenry was as expected. First Maccabees describes the flight of some of the residents of Jerusalem, who could not tolerate the introduction of foreign practices into the holy city.

> On every side of the sanctuary they shed innocent blood; they even defiled the sanctuary. Because of them the residents of Jerusalem fled; she became a dwelling of strangers; she became strange to her offspring, and her children forsook her. (1 Macc 1:37–38; cf. 2 Macc 5:27)

## THE BEGINNINGS OF THE HASMONEAN REVOLT 167 B.C.

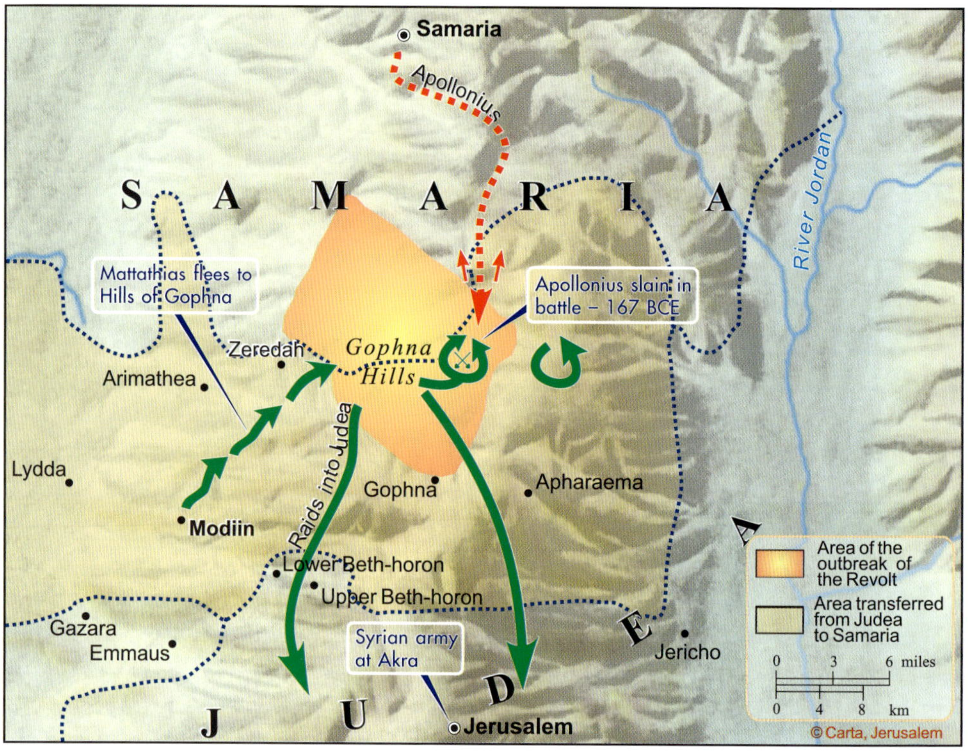


The author of First Maccabees observes that not everyone was disturbed by the new developments. "Many even from Israel gladly adopted [Antiochus'] religion; they sacrificed to idols and profaned the Sabbath" (1 Macc 1:43). Yet, for most of the citizens, even the assured penalty of death could not persuade them to profane the holy covenant and heed the king's edict. Scholarship has debated the origin and intent of Antiochus IV Epiphanes' harsh decrees. Certainly, his intolerance towards Jewish piety is exceptional when compared with the king's dealings with other peoples in his kingdom.

> And the king sent letters by messengers to Jerusalem and the cities of Judah; he directed them to follow customs strange to the land, to forbid burnt offerings and sacrifices and drink offering in the sanctuary, to profane Sabbaths and feasts, to defile the sanctuary and the priest, to build altars and sacred precincts and shrines for idols, to sacrifice swine and unclean animals, and to leave their sons uncircumcised. They were to make themselves abominable by everything unclean and profane, so that they should forget the law and change all the ordinances. And whoever does not obey the command of the king shall die. (1 Macc 1:44–50)

The aftermath of the royal decree is described in First and Second Maccabees and by Josephus (*Ant.* 12:248–256). According to First Maccabees 1:54, on the fifteenth of Kislev in 167 B.C., a desecrating sacrilege (cf. Dan 12:11) was set upon the altar with the sacrifice of unclean animals in the sanctuary of Jerusalem. The temple in Jerusalem was now consecrated to Zeus Olympius. Other altars were built around the country and books of the law were burned (1 Macc 1:54–55). If a person was found in possession of the law or discovered to still practice it, the penalty was death (1 Macc 1:57). Even women who circumcised their sons were executed (1 Macc 1:60).

Antiochus could not have known that his edicts would have unintended consequences. Rather than accelerating the Hellenization of the people of Judea, the forceful imposition of foreign customs and institutions solidified opposition to Seleucid rule and eventually led to the liberation of the Jewish nation.

CHAPTER 3

# JERUSALEM AND THE HASMONEANS

OVER THE NEXT CENTURY Jerusalem would lay at the epicenter of the story of the Hasmoneans. I will not here delve into great detail about the events of this fascinating period of Jewish conquest and reign. I have already presented a longer treatment in *The Sacred Bridge: Carta's Atlas of the Biblical World*. Instead, what is important for our present concerns are the salient portions that pertain to the history of Jerusalem, particularly those that contributed to the physical development of the city. For the most part, our presentation of the city walls and significant construction during the Hasmonean kingdom will be included in our consideration of Herodian Jerusalem. Many of the contributions by these priest kings remained in place after their power had passed to Herod the Great. Instead, a brief sketch will be given of the events that led up to Rome's conquest of Jerusalem and the rule of its client king, Herod.

The desecration of Jerusalem's temple spurred the priest Mattathias and his five sons to rise up against Antiochus IV. Their response to the Seleucid's Hellenizing efforts was quick and forceful. The writings of Josephus and First Maccabees recount that Matthathias son of John, a priest and leader from the village of Modiin (el-Midya; Eus. *Onom.* 132:16) near Lydda, was one of the first to refuse the king's edict (*Ant.* 12:265–271).

Employing guerrilla tactics in a series of skirmishes in the Judean hill country the Hasmoneans challenged Seleucid control of the population. Over the next three years Judas Maccabeus led his brothers in their struggle to liberate Jerusalem. Of particular importance were the strategic victories at Beth-horon (1 Macc 3:13–24; 2 Macc 8:1–7; *Ant.* 12:288–292) and Emmaus (1 Macc 3:38–4:25; 2 Macc 8:8–29; *Ant.* 12:293–312), because these challenged the historic northern and western access route from the coastal plain to Jerusalem via the Beth-horon ridge. The shocking defeats of the Seleucid forces at the hands of the band of rebels caught the attention of Antioch.

After the decisive battle at Beth-zur, Lysias, commanding general of the Seleucid forces, withdrew and returned to Antioch, "where he remained to enlist mercenaries and make preparations to invade Judea with a greater army" (*Ant.* 12:315). According to First Maccabees, with Lysias' retreat Judas proceeded to Jerusalem to begin the task of purifying the temple.

> So all the army assembled and went up to Mount Zion. There they saw the sanctuary desolate, the altar profaned, and the gates burned. In the courts they saw bushes sprung up as in a thicket, or as on one of the mountains. They saw also the chambers of the priests in ruins.... [Judas] chose blameless priests devoted to the law, and they

cleansed the sanctuary and removed the defiled stones to an unclean place. They deliberated what to do about the altar of burnt offering, which had been profaned. And they thought it best to tear it down, so that it would not be a lasting shame to them that the Gentiles had defiled it. So they tore down the altar, and stored the stones in a convenient place on the temple hill until a prophet should come to tell what to do with them. (1 Macc 4:37–46)

As the historical sources indicate, the retaking of Jerusalem was decisive but not the end of the struggle for freedom from Seleucid domination. Most historians mark true Jewish independence

**JERUSALEM IN THE HASMONEAN PERIOD 164–141 B.C.**

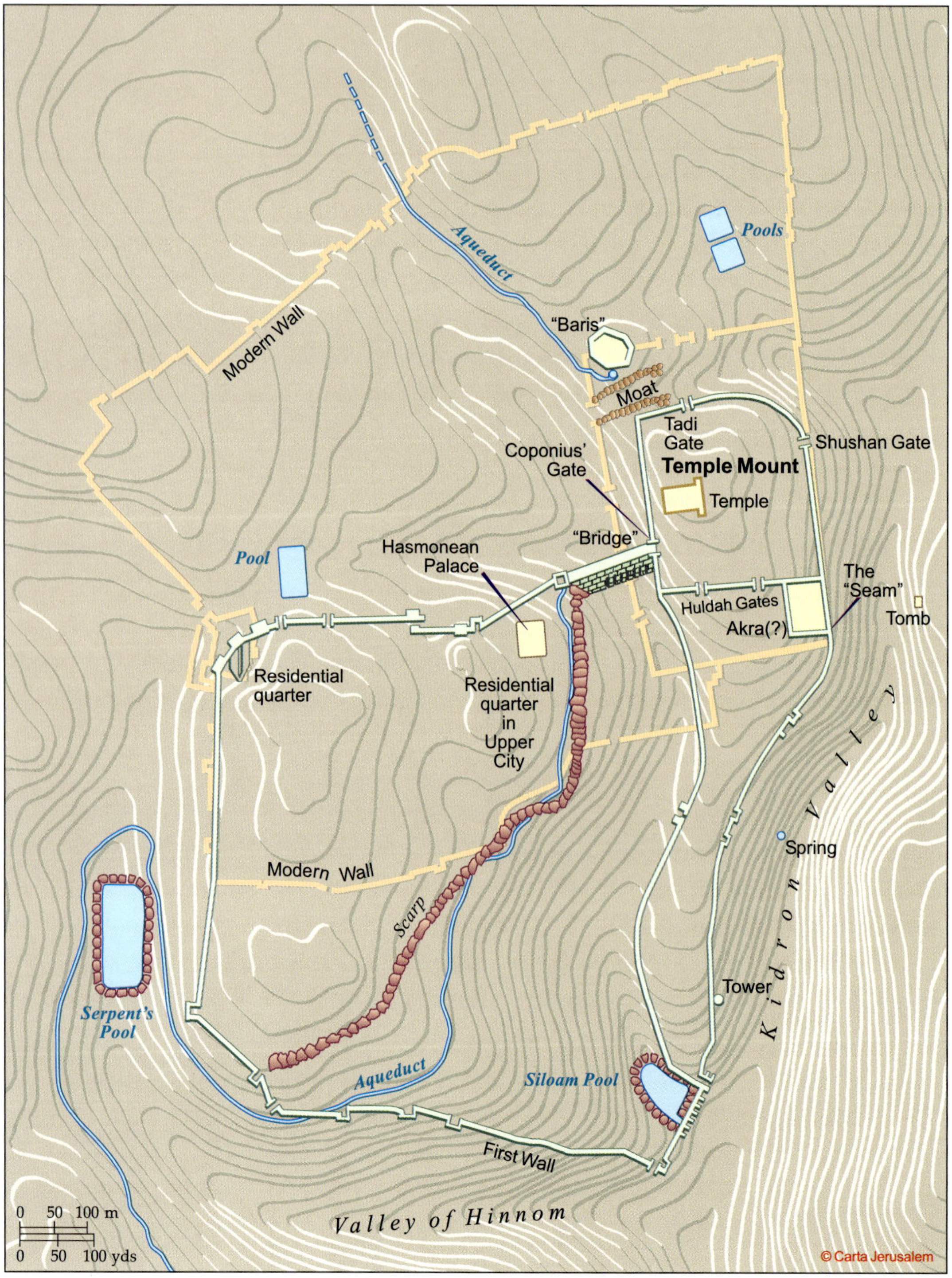

with the rule of Simon son of Mattathias in 141 B.C. The new era for Judea marked not only Simon's assumption of the high priesthood but liberation demonstrated by the relinquishment of Seleucid taxation upon the people of Judea. "This liberation and exemption from tribute came to the Jews in the hundred and seventieth year of the Syrian kingdom" (*Ant.* 13:213). Tyre and Sidon likewise established their eras from the beginning of their freedom from Seleucid rule.

### THE BATTLE OF BETH-ZUR AND THE REDEDICATION OF THE TEMPLE 165 B.C.

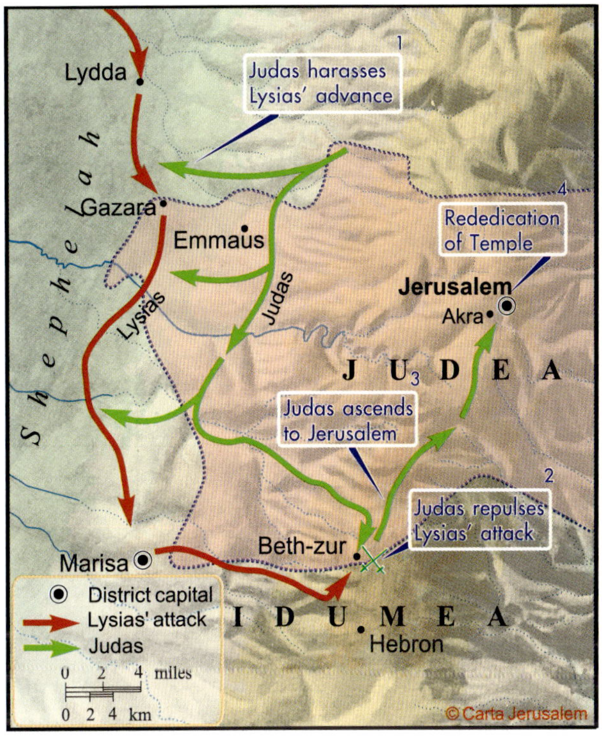


The last vestige of Antiochus IV Epiphanes' Hellenizing efforts was the Akra in Jerusalem. No Hasmonean leader had successfully vacated the fortress. The strategy of blockading the occupants within the fortress, which had begun under Jonathan, achieved its objective during the rule of his brother, Simon. According to First Maccabees, some of the occupants inside died of starvation. "Then they cried to Simon to make peace with them, and he did so. But he expelled them from there and cleansed the citadel from its pollution" (1 Macc 13:50; cf. *Meg. Ta'an.* 23 Iyyar).

Both First Maccabees and Josephus depict the surrender of the Akra. Josephus also supplies details of Simon's subsequent actions against the symbol of the pro-Greek faction in Jerusalem.

> [Simon] also took the citadel at Jerusalem by siege, razing it to the ground that it might not serve his foes as a base to occupy and do mischief from it, as they were then doing. Having done this, he thought it would be an excellent thing, and to his advantage to level also the hill on which the citadel stood, in order that the temple might be higher than this.…And so they all set to and began to level the hill, and without stopping work night or day, after three whole years brought it down to the ground and the surface of the plain.
>
> (*Ant.* 13:215–217; cf. *J.W.* 5:139)

The location of the Akra is still a matter of debate. No physical evidence of the dismantling of the Akra or the leveling of the place on which it stood has been identified among the modern excavations in the area of the Temple Mount. Josephus' claim that Simon utterly destroyed the Akra disagrees with the report of First Maccabees that Simon, "settled Jews in [the Akra], and fortified it for the safety of the country and of the city, and built the walls of Jerusalem higher" (1 Macc 14:37).

Not only was the last vestige of Seleucid control of Jerusalem removed, but the current ruler Antiochus VII Sidetes granted the citizens of Judea wide concessions.

> I confirm to you all the tax remissions that the kings before me have granted you, and release from all the other payments from which they have released you. I permit you to mint your own coinage as money for your country, and grant freedom to Jerusalem and the sanctuary. All the weapons that you have prepared and the strongholds that you have built and now hold shall remain yours. Every debt you owe to the royal treasury and any such fu-

*Coin of Antiochus VII Sidetes.* (photo Classical Numismatic Group, Inc. http://www.cngcoins, via Wikimedia Commons)

ture debts shall be canceled for you from henceforth and for all time. (1 Macc 15:5–8)

We are informed that Simon was granted the right to mint coins (1 Macc 15:6), a significant act denoting political independence. However, no coins from the time of Simon have yet been discovered, which has led some to question the reliability of the account. In any event, Antiochus would eventually reverse his attitude towards Simon and Judea, and this would lead to renewed armed conflict.

Simon was followed as ruler by his son, John Hyrcanus. He had little time to consolidate power, because Antiochus VII Sidetes invaded Judea in the first year of Hyrcanus' rule and ravaged the country (*Ant.* 13:236). The refortification of the western hill aided the Hasmoneans to temporarily withstand the siege of Antiochus VII Sidetes in 134–132 B.C. "At first he accomplished nothing whatever because of the strength of the walls and the valor of the besieged" (*Ant.* 13:237). Josephus' passing mention of the scarcity of water for the Seleucid troops during the siege may indicate that the waters of the Gihon that flow through Hezekiah's Tunnel into the Pool of Siloam were within the city walls in that day, and thus inaccessible to the Jerusalem attackers (*Ant.* 13:237). In the end the Syrian prevailed, and part of the peace treaty reached between John Hyrcanus and Sidetes entailed the dismantling of the fortifications that defended Jerusalem. The blockade also ended upon the condition that Hyrcanus agree to pay tribute for "Joppa and the other cities bordering on Judea" (*Ant.* 13:246). This concession was an acknowledgement that the cities belonged to the Seleucid kingdom. Rather than challenging the militarily superior king, the Hasmonean decided to wait for the inevitable change in power in Antioch to reassert his claim at a time (and under conditions) more advantageous to Judea.

Sidetes also demanded the return of a Seleucid garrison to Jerusalem, but Hyrcanus refused. Unlike Joppa and the cities on the borders of Judea, there had never been a question about Judea's claim to Jerusalem. It was recognized as an integral part of Judea and administrated by the high priest. The high priest countered the king with an offer of hostages to guarantee that no further insurrection would originate from Jerusalem or Judea. Before their departure the Seleucids pulled down the walls or battlements (*Ant.* 13:247; cf. Diod. Sic. 31.1; *Meg. Ta'an.* 21 Kislev) of the city.

Three years later in 129 B.C. Sidetes died at the hands of the Parthians, and his kingdom disintegrated. John Hyrcanus assumed that Seleucid attention would now be distracted by the Parthian threat from the east and the question of the succession of power in Antioch. He led military campaigns into the Transjordan, Samaria and Idumea. During this time he also rebuilt the walls of Jerusalem (1 Macc 16:23). His efforts to strengthen Jerusalem's defenses continued into the lengthy reign of his son, Alexander Jannaeus (103–76 B.C.).

In Antioch a dizzying series of changes kept the empire preoccupied with the succession of power. "The war between them gave Hyrcanus leisure to exploit Judea undisturbed with the result that he amassed a limitless sum of money" (*Ant.* 13:273). With the diversion of attention in Syria, Hyrcanus pursued military campaigns beyond the borders of Judea. He attacked Shechem and

Mount Gerizim in Samaria, site of the Samaritan temple (2 Macc 6:2; cf. *Meg. Ta'an.* 21 Kislev). He also subdued Idumea taking Adora and Marisa. In an unprecedented step, he allowed them to remain in their country, if they would agree to submit to circumcision "and were willing to observe the laws of the Jews" (*Ant.* 13:257). Proselytism on such a scale was unprecedented in the ancient world. Nevertheless, "from that time on they continued to be Jews" (*Ant.* 13:258).

In contrast to his father, the reign of Judah Aristobulus was the briefest of the Hasmonean dynasty (104–103 B.C.). Little is recorded of his accomplishments, saving only an incursion to the foothills of Mount Hermon where he subdued the Itureans, and in a gesture similar to his father allowed them, "if they wished to remain in their country, to be circumcised and to live in accordance with the laws of the Jews" (*Ant.* 13:318).

The Hasmonean kingdom reached its largest expanse under the younger son of John Hyrcanus, Alexander Jannaeus (103–76 B.C.). Yet, his external successes stand in stark contrast to the internal upheaval in Judea. A six-year civil war broke out with a large loss of life. Josephus' estimate of fifty thousand dead may be inflated, but it underscores the seriousness of the conflict. So desperate were those who opposed Jannaeus that they even sought the intervention of the Seleucid king, Demeterius III Akairos.

Demetrius was victorious in battle, but his success engendered sympathy for Jannaeus among the Hasmonean's Jewish opponents. Josephus implies that it is for this reason Demetrius withdrew to Syria. Jannaeus subsequently besieged the city where those who continued the struggle against him were held up. He overwhelmed them and brought them as captives to Jerusalem, where Josephus recounts a horrifying episode. In the only record of a Jewish ruler executing by crucifixion,

*The remains of the Byzantine church on Mount Gerizim built over the ruins of the Samaritan temple, which the Hasmonean John Hyrcanus destroyed in 108 B.C.* (photo Milner Moshe, via Wikimedia Commons)

Jannaeus hung eight hundred men and slaughtered their wives and children before their dying eyes. All the while, the king feasted with his concubines and watched the carnage. Although earlier scholarship cast doubt on the reliability of Josephus' record, this event is likewise remembered in the Qumran commentary *Pesher Nahum* on Nah 2:12 (4Q169 f3–4i:6–8).

At the time of his death Alexander Jannaeus ruled the whole of the coastal plain from the Kishon to the Brook of Egypt (excluding Ascalon), the whole of the mountains west of the Jordan from Dan to Beersheba, almost the whole area east of the Jordan from Paneas down to Zoar and the brook Zered. He had thus virtually restored the kingdom of David and Solomon.

The final decades of Hasmonean rule in Judea witnessed a bitter contest between the descendants of Alexander Jannaeus (103–76 B.C.) and Alexandra Salome (76–67 B.C.). Alexandra's death brought open conflict between their two sons, John Hyrcanus II and Judah Aristobulus II. Their struggle would continue and divide the nation until the arrival of the Romans at the gates of Jerusalem led by the general Pompey in 63 B.C.

> Pompey pitched his camp on the north side of the temple where it was open to attack. But even here stood great towers, and a trench had been dug, and the temple was surrounded by a deep ravine; for there was a steep slope on the [western] side toward the city after the bridge was destroyed, and at this spot Pompey by great labor day by day had caused earthworks to be raised. (*Ant.* 14:60–61)

The Romans built the siege structures virtually unopposed, because they took advantage of the restrictions on defensive actions by Jews on the Sabbath, "for the Law permits us to defend ourselves [on the Sabbath] against those who begin a battle and strike us, but it does not allow us to fight against an enemy [on the Sabbath] that does anything else (*Ant.* 14:63; *J.W.* 1:145–147; Dio Cass. 37.16.2). Pompey conquered the Temple Mount in the third month of the siege (*Ant.* 14:66; cf. *J.W.* 1:149) "on the *Feast Day*" (cf. Strabo *Geog.* 16.2.40; Dio Cass. 37.16.4) and entered the sanctuary.

Josephus reports that Pompey and his men entered the Holy of Holies but touched nothing (cf. Cic. *Flac.* 67; *Pss. Sol.* 2:1–2; 8:16–26; *contra* Dio Cass. 37.16.4). Later, Jewish opinion would interpret Pompey's violent death in Egypt as divine judgment for his hubris in entering the Holy of Holies, where only the high priest was permitted on the Day of Atonement (*Pss. Sol.* 2:25–31). Little physical damage was done to the temple, as testified by Josephus' report that Pompey ordered the temple to be ritually purified on the following day (*Ant.* 14:73). Then the Romans reinstalled John Hyrcanus II as high priest (*Ant.* 14:73; *J.W.* 1:153; cf. Dio Cass. 37.16).

*The* Pesher Nahum *scroll from Qumran.*

*Marble bust of Pompey, 17th century, Florence, Italy; on display in Chateau de Vaux-le-Vicomte, France.* (photo Jebulon, via Wikimedia Commons)

Pompey appointed a series of commanders to govern the region from Syria to Egypt, but none took such an active engagement of the internal affairs of Judea as Gabinius (*Ant.* 14:82). He divided the region into five districts (*Ant.* 14:91; *J.W.* 1:170) ruled from central cities: Jerusalem for Judea, Amathus for Perea, Jericho for the Jordan Valley and Sepphoris for Galilee. Scholars have debated the identity of the fifth city. However, there seems little question that Adora was intended. It was left as the most important city of eastern Idumea, a distinct region that remained attached to Judea during the Roman period.

Against the backdrop of Roman administration in Judea, two interwoven narratives unfolded that would have consequences into the following century. The sons of Judah Aristobulus II, Alexander and Antigonus, continued their armed resistance against Roman rule and its proxy John Hyrcanus II. At the same time, another figure, Antipater the governor of the district of Idumea repeatedly is mentioned because of his assistance and support for Rome both in Judea and abroad. He was rewarded with Roman citizenship (*Ant.* 4:137–138) and elevated from administrator (*Ant.* 14:127) to procurator of Judea (*Ant.* 14:43).

Antipater took advantage of his new position to place his two sons as governors, Phasael in Jerusalem and Herod in Galilee. In 40 B.C. Parthian forces invaded Syria to challenge Rome's eastern frontier. At considerable political risk, Antigonus approached the Parthians with a proposal for a political and military alliance against Rome (*Ant.* 14:331–333; *J.W.* 1:257). In a quick series of events, the Parthians captured Hyrcanus II and Phasael, later executing the son of Antipater.

Herod escaped by way of Masada to the Arabian capital of Petra, where he sought the support of the Nabatean king, Malchus. From there he traveled to Rhinocorura (Polyb. 5.80.3; Diod. Sic. 1.60.5; Strabo *Geog.* 16.1.12, 31; 16.4.24; Pliny *Nat. Hist.* 5:68) at the Brook of Egypt. Here he got word of Phasael's death (*Ant.* 13:374; *J.W.* 1:277). He continued to Alexandria, and he secured passage to Rome by ship.

In Rome, Herod found ready allies in Octavian and Mark Antony, who both had been assisted by Herod's father, Antipater (*Ant.* 14:127–136; 14:326). The Senate was convened to consider the events in Judea. The alliance between Antigonus and the Parthians had made him an enemy of Rome (*Ant.* 14:384). Mark Antony urged the Roman Senate that in light of the Parthian threat from the east it would be advantageous to have Herod on the throne. Herod's loyalty to Rome was well known. The Senate thus proclaimed in the summer of 40 B.C. that Herod should be king of Judea, and it granted to Herod the possessions of Hyrcanus II: Judea, Joppa, eastern Idumea, Perea, Galilee and the Jezreel Valley (*Ant.* 14:91; *J.W.* 1:170).

## NEW TESTAMENT JERUSALEM

CHAPTER 4

# Herodian Jerusalem

The decision by the Roman Senate to award Herod the throne of Judea did not materialize immediately (cf. *Ant.* 14:379–389; *J.W.* 1:282–285; Strabo *Geog.* 16.2.46; Tac. *Hist.* 5:9; App. *Bell. civ.* 5:75). After mustering an army of mercenaries, Herod set sail for Ptolemais (*Ant.* 14:394). The reception for the new monarch was mixed. Many had grown tired of the internecine fighting of the Hasmoneans. So, some locals welcomed him. Others saw in Herod a puppet of Rome. Still others considered his Idumean ancestry a disqualification for sitting on the throne of David (*Ant.* 14:403). This internal dissent would continue throughout Herod's reign.

Herod's balancing act—being both king of the Jews and a friend of Rome—is most clearly pictured in his building projects. He introduced emperor worship into his kingdom and constructed temples in honor of his benefactor, Caesar Augustus (*J.W.* 1:407; cf. *Ant.* 15:328–329) in cities named for the emperor: Caesarea (*J.W.* 1:414; *Ant.* 15:339), Sebaste (i.e., Samaria; *Ant.* 15:292–298) and Paneas (*Ant.* 15:363–364; *J.W.* 1:404–405; later re-named Caesarea Philippi: *Ant.* 18:28; *J.W.* 2:168). Complementing these Herod built three Jewish shrines to mark sites of importance in the life of Abraham, father of the nation and patron of proselytes (cf. *t. Bik.* 1:4, 64a): Machpelah, the tomb of the patriarchs in Hebron (*Ant.* 1:237, 256; Eus. *Onom.* 6:8; cf. Gen 23:1–20), Mamre (*Ant.* 1:196; Jub. 29:17, 19: 37:14, 17; cf. Eus. *Onom.* 124:5; cf. 6:8; Gen 13:14–18), and the temple in Jerusalem (*J.W.* 5:184–237; cf. 2 Chr 3:1).

Modern archaeological investigations indicate that all three of the Jewish shrines share a similar layout, employing a *temenos* design with walled, open-air precincts and a central sanctuary. Although the Herodian structures adopted some Greco-Roman architectural features, their enclosed sanctuaries—like those at Amrit, Baalbek, Palmyra and Damascus—were distinctive to the east. Despite their shared Herodian architectural characteristics, Josephus omits any reference to the sanctuaries at Hebron and Mamre. Instead, he writes at length solely about the monumental Herodian temple in Jerusalem (*J.W.* 5:184–237).

Herod refashioned Jerusalem into a bicameral city. On both its eastern and western hills, Herod built large walled enclosures, fortified on their northern approaches. On the eastern hill lay the site of the ancient temple, surrounded by a large open court and walls unparalleled in scale in the Roman Empire. Entrance from the north was guarded by the Antonia Fortress, named for Herod's friend and early supporter, Mark Antony (*Ant.* 15:292, 409; 18:91; *J.W.* 1:401; 5:238–247; Tac. *Hist.* 5:11). A similar open-air enclosure dominated the higher western hill—a neighborhood that Josephus describes as "the upper city" (*Ant.* 14:477; *J.W.* 1:39, 402; 2:344; *et passim*). Within its walls was Herod's royal residence. Three monumental towers guarded the northern entrance to the palace (*J.W.* 2:439; 7:1), each named for individuals significant in Herod's life: Mariamne, his Hasmonean wife; Hippicus, his friend and general (*J.W.* 5:163); and Phasael, Herod's brother who was murdered by the Parthians (*Ant.* 14:367, 379). The lower portions of the ancient tower in the modern-day Citadel in the Old City of Jerusalem belong to the tower of Phasael.

*The modern-day Citadel identified with the tower of Phasael* (photo Zachary Wong)

## THE WALLS OF HERODIAN JERUSALEM

Extensive excavations in Jerusalem over the past century have shed light on the expansion of the city during the Hasmonean and Herodian periods. Still under Persian domination, Nehemiah's rebuilding efforts were restricted to the restoration of walls on the city's eastern hill (Neh 2–3). Three centuries later, descriptions about the fortifying of Jerusalem are still confined to this area. Judas Maccabeus (1 Macc 4:60), Jonathan (1 Macc 10:11) and Simon (1 Macc 13:52) all are reported to fortify Mount Zion—the eastern hill. Yet, full political independence gained under the Hasmoneans (140–37 B.C.) resulted in a reinvigorated and enlarged Jewish capital in Judea. Jonathan extracted concessions from Demetrius I Soter to finance enhanced fortifications of the city (1 Macc 10:45). After Jonathan's untimely death at the hands of Trypho (1 Macc 13:23–24), Simon completed the initiative of his brother (1 Macc 13:10). "He settled Jews in [the city], and fortified it for the safety of the country, and of the city, and built the walls of Jerusalem higher" (1 Macc 14:37). Although First Maccabees speaks clearly about the contributions each of these rulers made to Jerusalem's walls, archaeologists are unable to identify which remnants of these walls were built by which Hasmonean rulers.

Since the Babylonian destruction of Jerusalem in 586 B.C., the wall built by Hezekiah encompassing the western hill had remained mostly in ruins. The Hasmoneans once again constructed a wall incorporating the western hill, approximating the eighth-century line and in places incorporating the ancient efforts into their new defenses. According to Josephus' testimony, it seems that residents of first-century Jerusalem were aware that portions of Hezekiah's wall had been incorporated into the later Hasmonean construction. So, the Jewish historian attributes the wall to the efforts of the earlier Davidic monarchy, "David, Solomon and their successors" (*J.W.* 5:143). At the same time, Josephus accurately traces the course of what he calls "the first wall" (*J.W.* 5:146; cf. 5:259–260, 301), a name that distinguished it from subsequent efforts.

> Beginning on the north at the tower called Hippicus, it extended to the Xystos, and then joining the council-chamber terminated at the western portico of the temple. Beginning at the same point in the other direction, westward, it descended past the place called Bethso to the gate of the Essenes, then turned southwards above the fountain of Siloam; thence it again inclined to the east towards Solomon's pool, and after passing a spot which they called Ophlas [i.e., the Ophel: 2 Chr 27:3; Neh 3:26], finally joined the eastern portico of the temple.
>
> (*J.W.* 5:144–145).

Extramural growth north of the walled city in the late Hasmonean period necessitated additional measures. A second wall was constructed to protect the burgeoning market area that extended north beyond the First Wall. No attribution is given for the building of the Second Wall, but it existed already at the time of Herod's siege of Jerusalem in 37 B.C., "The first wall was taken in forty days, and the second in fifteen more" (*Ant.* 14:476). So, it seems that the Second Wall was raised in the late Hasmonean period.

It should be noted that Josephus here reverses his designation for the walls (i.e., first, second, etc.) in the description of Herod's siege of Jerusalem. Rather than labeling the walls in the chronological order in which they were built, he reckons them in the order that the city's attackers encountered them. So, also in the Roman assault on Jerusalem in A.D. 70, the final wall completed by King Agrippa II in A.D. 66—elsewhere called the Third Wall (*J.W.* 5:147)—on this occasion he designates "the first wall" (cf. *J.W.* 5:302).

While modern archaeology has been prevented from determining the line of the Second Wall for lack of excavations in the densely populated Muslim and Christian Quarters of the Old City, Josephus indicates the wall's beginning and end. "The second wall started from the gate in the first

*The Roman gate underneath the Damascus Gate. Some of the stones in this complex remain* in situ *and date from the early Roman period.* (photo Deror Avi, via Wikimedia Commons)

*Stone (foreground) suggested by scholars to be part of the Third Wall.* (photo Paul. H. Wright)

wall which they call Gennath, and enclosing only the northern district of the town, went up as far as Antonia" (*J.W.* 5:146). Excavations in Jerusalem's Jewish Quarter in the 1970s identified the likely vicinity of the Gennath Gate, near where the Second Wall began. The location of the Antonia Fortress (*J.W.* 5:238–245) has long been understood to lie near the northwest corner of the Temple Mount, where it replaced an earlier citadel called the Baris that existed from the days of Nehemiah (Neh 2:8; 7:2) through the Hasmonean period (*Ant.* 13:307; 15:403).

Additional investigations below the Ottoman period Damascus Gate may also have uncovered evidence of the Second Wall. A triple-arched Roman gate belongs to Hadrian's Jerusalem—Aelia Capitolina (c. A.D. 135). Yet, it was built of reused Herodian ashlars. Nearby excavators found a single surviving course of large ashlar blocks that belonged to an earlier tower with an obtuse angle. Michael Avi-Yonah suggested that these stones were part of a gate tower, perhaps one of fourteen towers described by Josephus in the Second Wall (*J.W.* 5:158).

The Second Wall is particularly important for Christians in determining whether the current Church of the Holy Sepulcher—traditional site of Jesus' death, burial and resurrection—was inside or outside of the walled city of Jerusalem. Notwithstanding the lack of certainty concerning the line of the Second Wall, unmistakable first-century Jewish tombs still visible within the Holy Sepulcher suggest that the site was outside of the city in Jesus' day. The Jewish prohibition to bury the dead within the walls of a city (cf. *m. B. Batra* 2:9) means that the Second Wall coursed somewhere east of the Church of the Holy Sepulcher—leaving the church's location outside of the city walls.

Unlike Josephus' First and Second walls of Jerusalem, the Third Wall did not exist in the time of Jesus. It was initiated by Herod's grandson, Agrippa I, in A.D. 44 and completed by the rebels, just prior to the outbreak of hostilities against Rome in the First Jewish Revolt in A.D. 66 (*Ant.* 19:326–327; *J.W.* 2:219). Josephus describes its course.

> The third [wall] began at the tower of Hippicus, whence it stretched northwards to the tower of Psephinus, and then descending opposite the monuments of Helena (queen of Adiabene and daughter of king Izates), and proceeding past the royal caverns it bent round a corner tower over against the so-called Fuller's tomb and joining the ancient rampart terminated at the valley called Kidron. (*J.W.* 5:147)

Most scholars associate the Third Wall with the remains identified first by Edward Robinson in 1838, almost 1,400 feet (427 m) north of Jerusalem's Old City walls. The east-west line of the foundations extends from today's Russian Compound in West Jerusalem to the American School of Oriental Research (Albright Institute) in East Jerusalem. Although the Third Wall may have greatly increased the fortified neighborhoods of Jerusalem, it did little to impede the advance

## THE SIEGE OF JERUSALEM IN A.D. 70

of Titus and the Roman legions in the summer of A.D. 70. After only fifteen days, the Romans breached the wall and advanced to the Second Wall in their assault on Jerusalem (*J.W.* 5:302).

## CHAPTER 5

# THE UPPER CITY

JOSEPHUS COINED THE TOPONYM UPPER CITY to describe the western hill of Jerusalem (*Ant.* 14:477; 15:318; *J.W.* 1:39; 2:344, 530; 5:11; *et passim*).

> The city was fortified by three walls, except where it was enclosed by impassable ravines, a single rampart there sufficing. It was built, in portions facing each other, on two hills separated by a central valley, in which the tiers of houses ended. Of these hills that on which the *upper city* lay was far higher and had a straighter ridge than the other; consequently, owing to its strength it was called by King David—father of Solomon the first builder of the temple—the Stronghold (2 Sam 5:7), but we call it the upper agora. (*J.W.* 5:136–137)

Contrary to the historian's assertion, modern archaeology has determined that the area of the western hill was not included in the Jebusite city or the City of David. It was first occupied in the days of Hezekiah, later abandoned in the wake of the destruction by Nebuchadnezzar and through much of the Persian period, and then resettled in the Hellenistic period. During the days of the New Testament, the Upper City was the location of Jerusalem's wealthy elite. King Herod and the ruling high priests followed the example set by the later Hasmonean rulers. On the western hill overlooking the temple they built for themselves homes of exquisite size and beauty.

## HEROD'S ROYAL PALACE (THE PRAETORIUM)

Little remains of Herod's palatial residence in Jerusalem. Recent excavations have uncovered a large swimming pool cut into bedrock that underscores the opulence of the Herodian living quarters. He built the palace about ten years after assuming the throne, and once he had consolidated his hold on power (c. 25 B.C.).

> And when Herod's affairs were again in good order and increasingly prosperous, he built a palace in the Upper City, in which he constructed exceedingly large, high rooms and decorated them in very costly fashion with gold, stones and colour-washes (*Ant.* 15:318)....[The palace] comprised two most spacious and beautiful buildings, with which the temple itself bore no comparisons; these he named after his friends, the one Caesareum, and the other Agrippeum (*J.W.* 1:402).

Our picture of the reception halls in Jerusalem named for Augustus and Marcus Agrippa is aided by a similar architectural design in Herod's third winter palace in Jericho. There also Josephus reports that Herod honored Augustus and Agrippa by attaching their names to structures (*J.W.* 1:407). Even the colored stone tiles that are part of Josephus' description of the Royal Palace in Jerusalem find a complement in Jericho (*J.W.* 5:178–179).

Spacious gardens were an essential component of Herod's palaces. In Jericho the waters from Wadi Qelt that intersected the winter residence nourished the sunken garden. Likewise, Josephus describes the idyllic setting of the interior of the Jerusalem palace.

> All around were many circular cloisters, leading one into another, the columns in each being different, and their open courts all of greensward; there were groves of various trees intersected by long walks which were bordered by deep canals, and ponds everywhere studded with bronze figures, through which the water was discharged, and around the streams were numerous cots for tame pigeons. (*J.W.* 5:180–181)

The dovecote (columbarium) in the Jerusalem palace follows the examples found at other similar Hasmonean and Herodian palaces (e.g., Masada, Jericho and Cypros).

The three towers that guarded the northern entrance were the most prominent element in Herod's Jerusalem palace. Strategically, their position here reflects the weakness of Jerusalem from the north, a military reality that also dictated the additional fortifications facing the northern approaches to the Temple Mount (i.e., the Baris and the Antonia Fortress). In his very detailed description, Josephus describes the three towers of Herod's Jerusalem palace.

> Now Hippicus, called after his friend, was quadrangular, its length and breadth being each twenty-five cubits, and to the height of thirty cubits it was solid throughout. But above this solid and compact mass of masonry was a reservoir, twenty cubits deep, to receive the rain-water, and over this a double-roofed chamber, twenty-five cubits high, with roofs of diverse colors, this again was crowned by turrets, two cubits, and battlements, three cubits high, so that the total altitude amounted to eighty cubits.
>
> The second tower, which he named Phasael after his brother, was of equal length and breadth, forty cubits each; forty cubits was also the height of its solid base. Above and around this ran a cloister, ten cubits high, protected by parapets and bulwarks. Over this and rising from the centre of the cloister was built another tower,

*Excavated remains of the large Herodian pool in the Citadel area.* (photo R. Steven Notley)

*Scale model of the three Herodian towers: Phasael, Hippicus and Mariamme, from left to right.* (photo Zachary Wong)

> apportioned into sumptuous apartments, including a bath, in order that nothing might be wanting to impart to this tower the appearance of a palace. Its summit was crowned with battlements and turrets, and its total height was about ninety cubits. In form it resembled the tower of Pharos that emits its beacon light to navigators approaching Alexandria, but in circumference it was much larger…
>
> The third tower, Mariamme—for such was the queen's name—was solid to a height of but twenty cubits, its breadth being also twenty cubits and its length the same. But its upper residential quarters were far more luxurious and ornate than those of the other towers, the king considering it appropriate that one named after a woman should so far surpass in decoration those called after men, as they outdid the woman's tower in strength. The total height of this last was fifty-five cubits. (*J.W.* 5:164–171)

When Herod's son Archelaus was deposed in A.D. 6, control of the Royal Palace was transferred to the Roman prefect. A Roman garrison is also recorded here on several occasions (e.g., *Legat.* 38). Most notably, during the Jewish Revolt against Rome, the palace was the site of treachery, which according to Josephus cemented the course of the conflict with Rome. In a negotiated truce, Menachem and his rebel compatriots assured the Roman garrison safe passage, if the soldiers would abandon the towers unarmed. They agreed, but no sooner had they left the protection of the towers than they were slaughtered. Although the loss of life for the Romans was minimal in number, Jerusalem awoke the next morning to the realization that the full force of a Roman response would soon be felt. "To add to its heinousness, the massacre took place on the Sabbath, a day on which from religious scruples Jews abstain even from the most innocent of acts (*J.W.* 2:456; cf. *Meg. Ta'an.* 17 Elul).

## THE HASMONEAN PALACE

While Herod's palace was the most prominent and frequently mentioned in first-century Jerusalem, the royal residence of the Hasmoneans preceded it. No physical remains from the earlier palace have yet been discovered. Yet, there is circumstantial evidence that points us to its general vicinity. As we have noted, archaeologists have determined that during the Persian and early Hellenistic periods, there was sparse settlement on the western hill of Jerusalem. Resettlement efforts only began in earnest in the later Hellenistic period, likely coinciding with the renewed freedom brought by the Hasmoneans. Construction on the western hill continued into the reign of Herod when it reached its pinnacle in expanse and grandeur.

Jonathan is the first Hasmonean reported to reside in Jerusalem. His move to Jerusalem came after Demetrius I Soter sought to establish a strategic alliance with the son of Mattathias to prevent his support of the Syrian's contender for the throne, Alexander Balas. "Demetrius gave him authority to recruit troops, to equip them with arms and to become his ally; and he commanded that the hostages in the Citadel should be released to him" (1 Macc 10:6). Alexander countered Demetrius' offer, and subsequently he won Jonathan over with his promise to appoint the Hasmonean to be high priest of the nation and to grant him the honorific title, "the king's friend" (1 Macc 10:20–21). It was during this competition for Jonathan's allegiance that the Hasmonean left his stronghold in Michmash and moved to Jerusalem.

> And Jonathan dwelt in Jerusalem and began to rebuild and restore the city. He directed those who were doing the work to build the walls and encircle Mount Zion with squared stones, for better fortification; and they did so.
>
> (1 Macc 10:10)

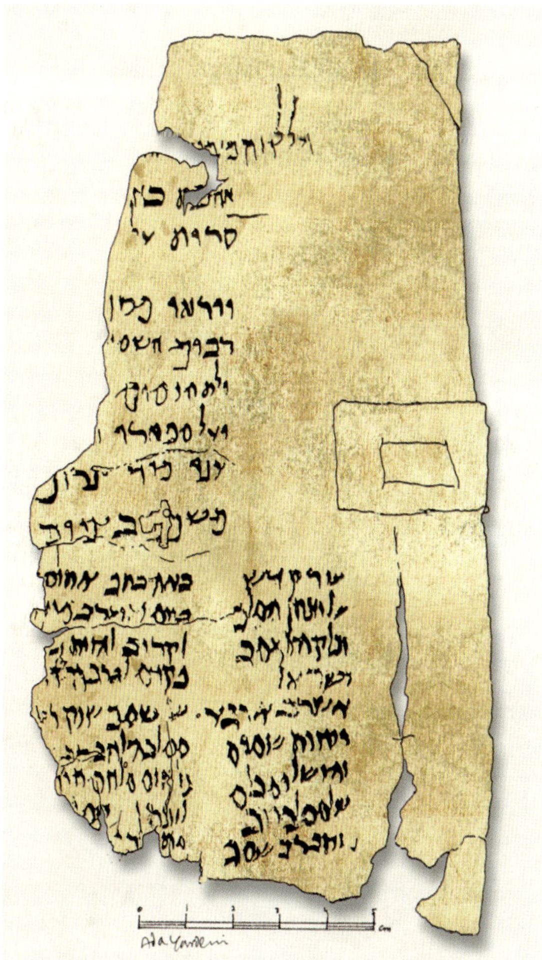

*A song for the welfare of Jonathan (Jannaeus) the King.* (Ada Yardeni)

The First Book of Maccabees makes no mention of where in Jerusalem Jonathan dwelt. Nor is there any early report of a Hasmonean palace. With the absence of physical evidence to determine the date of its construction, we are left to speculate about the palace's absence from reports concerning the days of Jonathan, Simon and John Hyrcanus. Later reports that Simon purified Gazara (Gezer) of its idols and built for himself a house there (1 Macc 13:43–48), may indicate that no formal residence for the first Hasmonean high priests existed in Jerusalem (cf. 1 Macc 13:52–53). Instead, perhaps the palace was constructed at the same time the Hasmonean rulers decided to take the title "king" in the days of Judah Aristobulus (*J.W.* 1:70) or Alexander Jannaeus (Strabo *Geog.* 16.2.40). Since Jerusalem's western hill had become the choice location for the wealthy, these aristocratic neighborhoods provided the likely setting *(right) Painted pottery from the Upper City, Jerusalem, Second Temple period.* (NEAEHL)

*(left) Coin of Alexander Jannaeus. Obverse: star in diadem "Yehonatan the king" in paleo-Hebrew between rays; reverse: anchor "of king Alexander" in Greek.* (Courtesy David Hendin)

for the site of the royal residence of the Hasmoneans.

In the final days of the last Hasmonean contender for the throne, Antigonus son of Aristobulus II, we hear about his siege of Jerusalem, "The men privately fell upon Jerusalem…they got together in great numbers and came against the king's palace and besieged it" (*Ant.* 14:334; cf. *J.W.* 1:250). His allies, the Parthians, also attacked the palace, "But when it was day, the Parthians plundered all Jerusalem, and the palace, and abstained from nothing but Hyrcanus' money, which was three hundred talents" (*Ant.* 14:363; *J.W.* 1:268).

The literary references to a royal palace in the days of the Hasmonean kingdom and modern archaeological findings of wealthy homes on the western hill set the backdrop for later historical indications of the continued existence of the Hasmonean palace on the western hill in the days of Agrippa II (A.D. 50–92). Josephus consistently distinguishes this palace with the topographical qualification, "near the colonnade" (i.e., the Xystos: *J.W.* 2:344; 4:581; 5:144; 6:191, 325, 377). It seems that the Hasmonean palace stood on the eastern slopes of the western hill overlooking the Temple Mount.

> About this time king Agrippa built a chamber of unusual size in his palace at Jerusalem near the colonnade. The palace had been erected long before by the sons of Asamonaios (i.e., the Hasmoneans) and, being situated on a lofty site, afforded a most delightful view to any who chose to survey the city from it. The king was enamoured of this view and used to gaze, as he reclined at meals there, on everything that went on in the temple.
>
> (*Ant.* 20:189–190)

Agrippa's presence in the Hasmonean palace corresponds with reports of the Roman governors in Herod's Royal Palace. When Archelaus, Herod's son, was deposed, administration of his territories passed directly to the Romans. The royal residences of Herod that had been inherited by Archelaus in Judea and Samaria became the official residences of the Roman principals. On the other hand, when members of the Herodian ruling dynasty (Antipas, Philip, Agrippa I, etc.) visited Jerusalem they stayed in the Hasmonean Palace overlooking the Temple Mount.

## THE WAY OF THE CROSS

The understanding of two co-existing palaces in Jerusalem assists to identify the location of Pilate and Herod Antipas during the tragic events surrounding Jesus' death. Normally the prefect resided in Caesarea, the center of Roman power in the province of Judea. However, to maintain a show of imperial power when the crowds gathered for Passover, Pilate came to Jerusalem. The official residence of the chief Roman magistrate was designated in Latin the *praetorium*.

In the case of the New Testament, the praetorium designated the royal residences of Herod the Great, which were now occupied by the Roman governor. In Caesarea this was Herod's Mediterranean villa. So, when the New Testament describes the arrest of Paul, it states that he was taken to the Roman governor's residence in Caesarea, which was aptly called "the praetorium of Herod" (Acts 23:35). In Jerusalem both Philo (*Legat.* 38:299) and Josephus (*J.W.* 2:31) record that Herod's palace in Jerusalem was likewise the residence of the Roman governor.

These contemporary extracanonical witnesses are important for our reading of the report of John 18:28: "Then they led Jesus from the house of Caiaphas to the praetorium." This is paralleled by Matthew 27:27: "Then the governor's soldiers took Jesus into the praetorium"; and even more poignantly in Mark 15:16: "The soldiers led Jesus away to the palace (that is, the praetorium)." In other words, all of the Gospels record that after a period of initial inquiry by the temple authorities (Caiaphas, Annas and other members of the temple establishment), Jesus was taken to the Roman prefect, Pontius Pilate, who was staying at Herod's Jerusalem palace (i.e., the praetorium), and they accused Jesus of political sedition (Luke 23:1–2).

Later medieval Christian tradition identified the location of Pilate with the Antonia Fortress, built by Herod the Great and named after his early benefactor, Mark Antony. However, the reports

*Coin of Herod Antipas.*

*The Pontius Pilate inscription from Caesarea, now on display at The Israel Museum, Jerusalem.* (photo Zachary Wong)

we have of Pilate's presence in Jerusalem place him consistently in the former palace of Herod the Great. It should also be noted that Mark's description that Jesus was led to "the palace" cannot have been the Antonia. Nowhere in the New Testament or other contemporary literature is the Antonia Fortress called a "palace."

In Josephus' *The Jewish War* 2:175–177 (*Ant.* 18:60–62), he tells of a riot caused by Pilate's taking funds from the temple treasury to pay for an aqueduct. We will not concern ourselves with the full details of this fascinating episode, but only note that it transpired in Herod's Palace and that Pilate received the crowd from a platform (*bema*) raised in the Royal Palace. It is not a coincidence that likewise in the condemnation of Jesus by Pilate in John 19:13, we find mention of a tribunal (*bema*). Another report is that related by Philo in his *Letter to Gaius* 38:299–305 about an offense by Pilate when votive shields with images were placed in the Royal Palace in Jerusalem. It occurred at the time of one of the pilgrimage festivals, and once again describes Pilate at the royal residence during a holiday.

Returning to John 19:13, the Evangelist describes that Pilate brought Jesus outside. He sat on a tribunal at a place called the Lithostratos. There has been considerable scholarly discussion regarding both the etymology of the Greek term and its location. Insufficient attention has been given to the late Ehud Netzer's archaeological discovery at Herod's winter palace in Jericho and the recent salvage investigation of debris from the Temple Mount under the direction of Gabriel Barkay and Zachi Dvira (see below). Both contribute to our understanding of Josephus' description of the Royal Residence in Jerusalem—particularly as it pertains to our understanding of the Greek term *lithostratos*.

Even prior to these discoveries, the main problem with the identification of the flagstones below the Church of Ecce Homo (site of the Antonia Fortress) with John's Lithostratos was their date. Excavators demonstrated conclusively that these stones date from the time of Hadrian (A.D. 135) and not from the New Testament period. In addition, scholars struggled to reconcile the identification of the flagstones with the sense of the Greek term that means pavement or mosaics.

The identification of the Praetorium with Herod's Royal Residence in Jerusalem opens some new possibilities for the etymological challenge of the *lithostratos*. Since little remains of Herod's palatial residence in Jerusalem, it is useful to revisit Josephus' description about the palace, because it contributes valuable information concerning the *lithostratos*.

> And when Herod's affairs were again in good order and increasingly prosperous, he built a palace in the Upper City, in which he constructed exceedingly large, high rooms and decorated them in very costly fashion with gold, stones and *colour-washes*. (*Ant.* 15:318)

Our picture of the Royal Palace in Jerusalem named for Augustus and Marcus Agrippa has now been illuminated by a similar architectural design in Herod's third winter palace in Jericho. There also Josephus reports that Herod honored Augustus and Agrippa by attaching their names to structures (*J.W.* 1:407). Even the colored stone tiles that are part of Josephus' description of the Royal Palace in Jerusalem find a complement in Jericho. In *The Jewish War* he describes the construction, "in which the variety of the stones is not to be expressed; for a large quantity of those that were rare of that kind was collected together" (*J.W.* 5:178).

Josephus' description of the variegated colored stones comprising the pavement at Herod's

*Opus sectile tiles found in the salvage dig from the Temple Mount. Josephus refers to these tiles in* J.W. *6:85–96 with the Greek word* lithostratos. *The discovery of similar opus sectile tiles in Herod's palace in Jericho indicates that this may have been the preferred Herodian style of pavement and is likely what was meant in John 19:13 by the* lithostratos *in Herod's Royal Palace in Jerusalem.* (photo Zachi Dvira; courtesy Gabriel Barkay)

palaces in Jerusalem and Jericho in light of the archaeological discoveries suggests a new understanding for John's mention of the Lithostratos in the Praetorium of Jerusalem; namely, that John's reference to the Lithostratos refers to the ornately tiled floors surrounding the two buildings Herod named in honor of his friends, Caesar Augustus and Marcus Agrippa.

Together with these literary and archaeological witnesses, we can now add the recent discoveries from the salvage investigation of debris from the Temple Mount. Barkay and Dvira have found ornate paving stones from the stone esplanade surrounding Herod's temple. These bear a striking resemblance to the colored stone floors from Jericho, and it is in his description of the paved courts of the Temple Mount where Josephus uses the Greek term *lithostratos*.

> Julian (a centurion from Bithynia) had shoes all full of thick and sharp nails, as had every one of the other soldiers, so when he ran on the *pavement* (*lithostratos*) *of the temple*, he slipped, and fell down upon his back with a very great noise, which was made by his armor. This made those that were running away to turn back; whereupon those Romans that were in the tower of Antonia set up a great shout, as they were in fear for the man.
>
> (*J.W.* 6:85–86; cf. 6:189)

The Gospel of John further describes the place of judgment with the term Gabbatha. This doubtless is a derivation of the Hebrew term *giḇᶜāh* for which we have numerous Old Testament toponymic examples—Gibeon, Geba and Gibeah. Its lemma means hill or elevated place and corresponds to Josephus' description that Herod's Palace was in the Upper City. This nomenclature was used to distinguish it from the Hasmonean palace somewhat lower on the western hill or other royal residences closer to the Temple Mount.

According to Luke 23:2 Jesus was charged with stirring up the population from Galilee to Jerusalem, encouraging the people not to pay taxes and claiming to be the king Messiah. When his accusers informed Pilate that he came from Galilee, the prefect recognized that Jesus belonged to the jurisdiction of Galilee. He sent Jesus to Herod Antipas, tetrarch of Galilee and Perea. As we have indicated, Herod's son would have been at the former Hasmonean palace only a couple hun-

*The triclinium in the northern wing of Herod's third winter palace at Jericho; the impressions of the opus sectile floor are clearly visible.* (NEAEHL)

dred meters away (*Ant.* 20:190; *Philonis* 301). Antipas had been seeking to meet Jesus face to face (Luke 13:31–33; 23:8), but at their encounter Jesus remained silent. It seems the tetrarch did not consider Jesus to be the threat his cousin John had been, so he returned the Galilean to Pilate in mocking attire (Luke 23:11–12).

Pilate attempted to punish Jesus and release him, but his Sadducean accusers who had been the target of Jesus' public rebuke pressed for his execution. The Roman prefect had a reputation, according to Philo, for his brutality, "a man of inflexible, stubborn and cruel disposition" guilty of "venality, violence, robbery, assault, abusive behavior, frequent executions without trial, and endless savage ferocity" (*Legat.* 301–302; cf. 303–305; *Ant.* 18:55–59; 60–62; *J.W.* 2:175–177).

David Flusser brought attention to one additional facet of Pilate's character. The Roman prefect's small temple built in Caesarea in honor of Tiberius is the only known temple built by a Roman official for a living emperor. Pilate's efforts to ingratiate himself to the emperor—who according to Suetonius (*Tiberius* 26) forbade temples dedicated to himself—reveals another aspect of the official's complex personality. He possessed a personal weakness precisely at the point of persuasion put forward by Jesus' accusers. John's Gospel provides a unique report about the tipping point for Pilate's condemnation of Jesus. They pressed, "If you release [Jesus], you are no friend of Caesar!" (John 19:12). Pilate condemned Jesus to death by crucifixion, and he was summarily led a short distance outside of the city to be executed.

Since the medieval period the *Via Dolorosa* ("the way of suffering") has been traced through the streets of Jerusalem, beginning at the site of the Antonia Fortress east of the Church of the

## THE ARREST, INTERROGATION AND EXECUTION OF JESUS

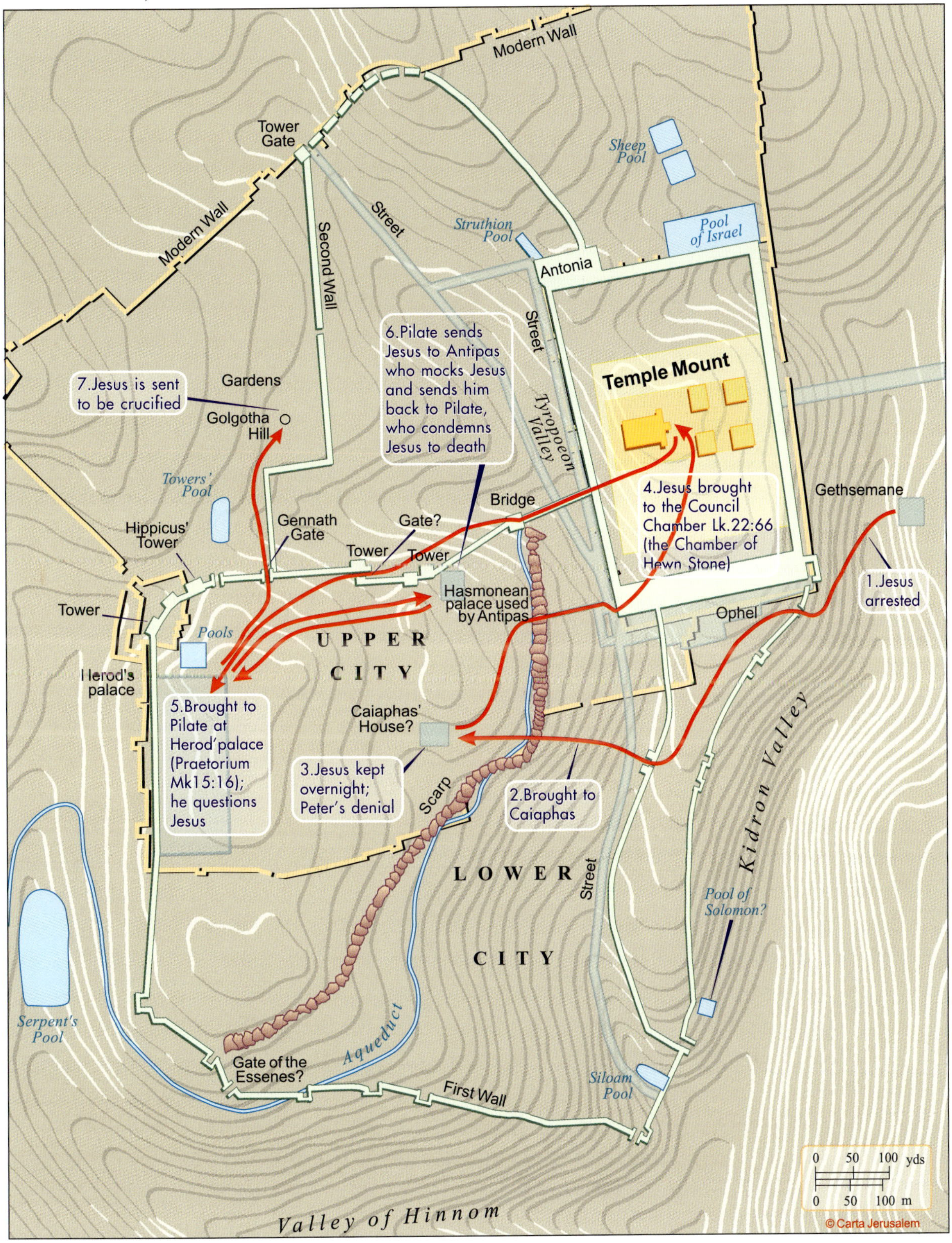


Holy Sepulcher. Yet, there are earlier Byzantine traditions that remember the place where Jesus was flogged on the western hill (Bordeaux Pilgrim 592). These Christian traditions have confusedly combined the event of Jesus' flogging with his brief confinement at the house of Caiaphas. The

*So-called Tomb of Joseph of Aramathea in the Church of the Holy Sepulcher.* (photo Peter Wong)

Gospels record that it was Pilate's soldiers who flogged Jesus, while he was still in the Praetorium (Matt 27:26; Mark 15:15). With the recognition that the Roman prefect was at Herod's former palace on the western hill, the Byzantine tradition may be a vestige of a pre-Byzantine memory concerning the location of Jesus' Roman incarceration, flogging and condemnation to death.

If these observations are correct, then the starting point for Jesus' way of suffering began on the western hill, today's Mount Zion. He was led from Herod's palace and through the northern city gate to be crucified. Excavations directed by the Israeli archaeologist Nahman Avigad south of the Muristan and on the northern edge of the Jewish Quarter in the Old City of Jerusalem discovered portions of the First Wall of Jerusalem described by Josephus. Even more importantly Avigad proposed in the vicinity the location of a first-century gate. Josephus records only one gate in this area along the northern line of the First Wall, the Gennath Gate: "The second wall started from the gate in the first wall which they called Gennath (i.e., Garden Gate), and (the second wall) enclosing only the northern district of the town, went up as far as Antonia" (*J.W.* 5:146). Avigad concluded that these remains should be identified with the Gennath Gate mentioned by Josephus.

If Jesus was taken from Herod's Palace to the area north of the walled city as Christian tradition remembers, then he may have been taken out of the city through the Gennath Gate. Josephus does not discuss the etymology of the name of the gate, but once again the Fourth Gospel may assist. It supplies a unique topographical detail about the area where Jesus was executed, "in the place where [Jesus] was crucified there was *a garden*" (John 19:41). John's description of an agricultural area north of the city corresponds to the etymology of the Gennath Gate. The gate opened northward beyond the First Wall of Jerusalem to an area of gardens. It is in this area that ancient Christian tradition marks the place of Jesus' death and burial.

Twenty years of investigations as part of restoration work within the Church of the Holy Sepulcher helped to determine the early history of the site. It was the location of a limestone quarry during the Old Testament period. Virgilio C. Corbo, who oversaw the investigation, claims that he found evidence the area was transformed into an orchard where fig trees, carob trees and olive trees were planted. This quarry-garden was later made a place of burial. At least four tombs from the turn of the era have been identified within the confines of the church.

Unfortunately, the traditional tomb of Jesus has been severely damaged over the centuries, and visitors can see little of the original hewn stone. Nevertheless, the so-called Tomb of Nicodemus and Joseph of Aramathea nearby is typical of a first-century *kokh* tomb. The site remains the best candidate for the place of Jesus' death, burial and resurrection. Certainly he was executed within the vicinity, and access from Herod's Palace, the Praetorium, would have led through the Gennath Gate— in all likelihood marking the line of the first-century Way of the Cross.

## RESIDENCES OF JERUSALEM'S PRIESTS

Excavations in the Jewish Quarter of the Old City of Jerusalem uncovered an inscribed weight measure from the home of Bar Kathros, another family of high priests. This family is remembered in the Babylonian Talmud in the context of criticisms towards high priestly dynasties from the Roman period. These priests were criticized for their oppression, secrecy and financial misconduct. In a saying remembered by the second generation *Tanna*, Abba Saul b. Batnit:

> Woe is me because of the house of Boethus;
> Woe is me because of their staves!
> Woe is me because of the house of Hanin (=Annas);
> Woe is me because of their whisperings!
> Woe is me because of the house of Kathros;
> Woe is me because of their pens!
> Woe is me because of the house of Ishmael the son of Phabi;
> Woe is me because of their fists!
> For they are High Priests and their sons are [temple] treasurers and their sons-in-law are trustees and their servants beat the people with staves
>
> (*b. Pesah.* 57a = *t. Menah.* 13:21)

Discovery of other monumental homes near to the Bar Kathros house has raised the possibility that this area may have been the neighborhood of other high priestly families. The size and elegance of these homes is notable. Each had at least one ritual immersion bath (*miqveh*) and some had several, indicating the residents' heightened concern for issues of ritual purity. One designated by the archaeologists "the Palatial Mansion" is remarkable. It was a multi-storied home, over 600 square meters (6,458 sq. ft.) in size. It contained imported vessels, and its plastered walls were covered with frescoes, newly refashioned to imitate contemporary Roman styles just prior to its destruction. A signature glass pitcher discovered within the ruins was the work of the renowned glassmaker, Ennion of Sidon. The residents of this mansion must have been a particularly wealthy and influential family. The number of ritual baths and its close proximity to the dwelling of the Bar Kathros family suggests that the house may have also belonged to a family of high priests. Although there is insufficient evidence to identify these palatial buildings as the homes of the high priestly figures mentioned in the New Testament, their size and rich decoration assists us to understand the social and economic status of those among the temple establishment who opposed Jesus.

## CHAPTER 6

# The Setting for the Last Supper

Almost seven decades have passed since a young Bedouin shepherd stumbled upon one of the most remarkable archaeological discoveries of the twentieth century—the Dead Sea Scrolls. After the publication of this ancient library, which belonged to those who dwelt at nearby Khirbet Qumran, we have a better understanding of their fascinating type of Jewish piety. The writings belong to the interwoven fabric of competing ideas that are important for our understanding of the varieties of ancient Judaism, as well as the shaping influences on early Christianity. While John the Baptist shares some similarities in thinking and expressions with the Qumran Congregation (their ablutions, their self-identification with the "Voice" in Isaiah 40:3, and their apocalyptic rhetoric), Jesus had little in common with this apocalyptic, separatist community.

The stark differences between Jesus and the Qumran Congregation have not stopped the endless speculation by those who seek to establish a direct link between Jesus and the Essenes—the likely identity of those who lived at Khirbet Qumran. Yet, the evidence of any connection between them remains so thin that the claim resembles what the rabbis might have deemed "a mountain hanging by a hair." Many of these proponents believe that Jesus' Last Supper was shared in an Essene enclave in Jerusalem. By doing so, they hope to underscore the Jewish roots of Christianity. While well intentioned, they have pursued the wrong path to a laudable end. In the words of David Flusser, the question is not whether Jesus was Jewish, but what kind of Jew was he?

The attempt to associate Jesus with the Qumran Congregation ignores the yawning gap that existed between the spiritual world of the sage from Galilee and the Essenes. Not only do we find Jesus unsympathetic to the worldview of the Essenes, at points he voices his strong opposition to it. "You have heard that it was said, 'You shall love your neighbor and hate your enemy.' But I say to you, Love your enemies..." (Matt 5:43–44). There is little question that Jesus here forcefully rebuts the ethic of sectarian hatred, which was a signature feature of Qumran ideology, "To love all whom [God] has chosen and to hate all whom he has rejected" (1QS 1:5).

Others find in the Dead Sea Scrolls answers to nagging questions that have dogged Christian readers for centuries. As is well known, John's Gospel parts company at points with the Synoptic Gospels in its historical description of the final days of Jesus. Two of John's variances have particular relevance to the Dead Sea Scrolls. Unlike the Synoptic Gospels, the Fourth Gospel lacks any historical details that specify the Last Supper was a Passover meal. In fact, it has become quite popular to question whether the Last Supper was a Passover meal at all.

Following a Qumranic line of reading John's Gospel, some suggest Jesus abandoned the appointed day for Passover observed in the temple, which adhered to the traditional Jewish lunar calendar, in order to follow the Essene solar calendar. According to this theory, he celebrated the festal meal two days earlier (i.e., Tuesday evening rather than Thursday). This creative proposal is intended to answer the chronological variance in the Gospels. While the Synoptic Gospels describe Jesus' death on the first day of the Feast of Unleavened Bread (i.e., the day following the Passover eve), John informs us that the Jewish feast had not yet begun (John 19:14; also 13:1). Instead, according to the timetable of the Fourth Gospel, Jesus' death coincided with the sacrifice of the Passover lamb on the eve of Passover (cf. John 19:33; LXX Exod 12:46).

Those familiar with the complex literary relationships between the four Gospels understand that reading the Fourth Gospel through the lens of the Qumran Congregation's solar calendar does not really reconcile the differences between John and the Synoptic Gospels. It merely dismisses the shorter, simpler chronology of the Synoptic Gospels in lieu of John's creative theological presentation of Christ as the paschal lamb. This approach mirrors the theological proclamation of the Apostle Paul, "Christ our Passover [lamb] has been sacrificed" (1 Cor 5:7). A similar interpretive thread between Passover and the figure of a beloved son is heard in the ancient Jewish commentary on Exodus, the *Mekilta de-Rabbi Ishmael*. The Jewish work sought to plumb the depths of the spiritual significance of the blood of the Passover lamb in the Exodus account. So, it posed a question about whose blood the Lord saw upon the lintel of the doorpost in Egypt:

> And when I see the blood (Exod 12:13). I see the blood of the sacrifice of Isaac. For it is said: "And Abraham called the name of that place Adonai-yireh (the Lord will provide [or, *see*])" (Gen 22:14).

The association between the death of the beloved son and the Passover lamb is neither a Johannine invention, nor a creation of the later Jewish interpreter of the *Mekilta*. These ideas are already heard in the second century B.C. in the Book of Jubilees 17:15, where Abraham is described to offer Isaac, his beloved son, *on the eve of Passover* (i.e., the 14th of Nisan)—a chronological detail not included in the biblical account. All of these examples belong to stylized historical retellings, whose narratives served their communities as vehicles to communicate deeply held religious beliefs. What is important to keep in mind, however, is that this style of midrashic or homiletical literature, i.e., the creative and expansive retelling of biblical stories, was intended to bring the reader's attention to spiritual content that was not apparent through a simple (*peshat*) reading of the biblical text. At the same time, this literary genre was never meant to be read as unvarnished history.

*Replica of a sundial found at Qumran.* (photo Peter Wong)

The problem with those who propose that John's theologically rich account be read through the lens of the Qumran solar calendar is that they argue Jesus *in fact* died on the eve of Passover. By doing so, they create an insurmountable impasse. The resort to the Essene solar calendar in the reading of the Gospels not only does not solve the chronological conundrum in the Passion narratives, it makes the matter worse. No harmonization of John and the Synoptic Gospels allows Jesus to celebrate the Passover and to be crucified on the same evening.

## IRRECONCILABLE CALENDARS

The deep divide between the solar and lunar calendars should not be minimized. In our account, it is not just a matter of two days. To embrace the solar calendar in the first century was to reject entirely the validity of the temple in Jerusalem. This is no small matter. Is this the impression we receive in the Gospels about Jesus and his followers? Is there collaborating evidence either to support or to challenge the notion that Jesus adopted the Essene preference for the solar calendar over the lunar calendar used in Jerusalem's temple? Did Jesus likewise share the Qumran Congregation's concomitant vilification of the temple? To accept that such a radical position was the opinion of Jesus requires more than inference.

First of all and most obvious, Jesus' pilgrimage to Jerusalem at the time of Passover makes absolutely no sense, if he shared the Essene rejection of the temple in Jerusalem. Jews were permitted to celebrate Passover outside of Jerusalem, and most in fact did so. Pilgrimage to the Holy City at the time of the biblical feast served for one reason only—to make possible the pilgrim's participation in the temple and to observe the Passover meal within the city walls.

During the week before Passover, Jesus stayed in Bethany (Mark 11:11). As the holiday approached he arranged for a room within the walls of the city to celebrate the Passover meal. The setting for the Last Supper within the walled city of Jerusalem is one of the most compelling arguments that the Last Supper was indeed a Passover meal. It was required that those who shared in the lamb sacrificed in the temple on the eve of Passover (the 14th of Nisan) ate it that very evening (Exod 12:10; *m. Zeb.* 5:8; *m. Pesah.* 10:9; cf. *m. Ber.* 1:1) and within the walls of Jerusalem (*m. Pesah.* 7:9, 12; 10:3).

The provision to eat the Passover lamb within the city walls was a practical accommodation to the spatial limits of the temple precincts. The sheer number of pilgrims did not allow the continuation of the earlier custom to eat the meal within the courts of the temple. The relaxing of this limitation by Israel's Sages is not the opinion shared by the Book of Jubilees, a work from the 2nd century B.C. that was found in the Qumran library:

> And in the days when the house has been built in the name of the Lord in the land of their inheritance, they shall go there and slay the passover in the evening, at sunset, at the third part of the day. And they shall offer its blood on the threshold of the altar, and shall place its fat on the fire that is upon the altar, and *they shall eat its flesh roasted with fire in the court of the house that has been sanctified in the name of the Lord.* (Jub 49:19–20)

This is also the instruction of the Temple Scroll, another Qumran work penned in the pre-Christian era, "Then they are to eat [the Passover] at night, in the courtyards of [the] temple. Afterwards they shall arise early in the morning and return home" (11QT 17:7–9). So, according to both Jubilees and the Temple Scroll, even if in the days of Jesus the Essenes had participated in the Passover sacrifice in Jerusalem (which they did not), they would have eaten the festive meal within the temple precincts and not on the western hill of today's Mount Zion, as is proposed by those who desire to locate an Essene quarter there. Instead, the Dead Sea Scrolls and the testimony of Josephus indicate that the Essenes, because of their rejection of the temple in the first century, had abandoned active participation in the temple sacrifices altogether—including the Passover.

On the other hand, what is assumed by the Evangelists in their Gospels is a detail so customary as to warrant no mention; namely, that shortly before the Passover meal, Jesus and those who accompanied him from Galilee ascended to the temple and sacrificed the paschal lamb. This was an offering routinely carried out by the people themselves and not the priests. While a portion of the victim would have been left for the sacrifice (Lev 3.3–4, *m. Pesah.* 5:10) most of the lamb was taken by the people and served at the festive meal.

*Detail of the Temple Scroll from Qumran.*

An indication that the paschal lamb sacrificed in the temple was part of the Last Supper is included in the words of Jesus, "I have earnestly desired to eat this *paschal lamb* (or *Passover*: *to pascha*) with you..." (Luke 22:15). Christian readers seldom recognize the idiomatic Hebraism in Luke's Greek saying. The name for the holiday (*pesach*) is likewise the term for the sacrificial offering served at the meal (*pesach*). To wit, modern translators render the identical Greek word in the Apostle Paul's declaration, "For Christ, our *Passover lamb* (*to pascha*; cf. Matt 26:17; Mark 14:12) has been sacrificed" (1 Cor 5:7).

If the Passover lamb was a part of the Last Supper, then it is impossible that Jesus' meal coincided with the Essene Passover, or that it would have been welcomed in an Essene enclave. The paschal lamb could be sacrificed only in the temple and only on the 14th of Nisan according to the lunar calendar used by the temple (Exod 12:6; *m. Pesah.* 5:3, 5). By contrast, the Essene Passover meal occurred that year two days earlier than the Passover celebrated in Jerusalem. In addition, because of the Essene boycott of the temple, there would have been no Passover lamb at the Tuesday evening meal of the Essenes. Neither of these details regarding Essene customs squares with the New Testament account of the Last Supper.

Two additional details about that meal demonstrate that the Passover of Jesus was not an Essene meal. Jesus and those who celebrated the biblical feast with him *reclined* (Matt 26:20; Mark 14:18). Even the Gospel of John, whose Passion chronology is read by some to suggest an Essene Passover, describes Jesus and those with him *reclining* (John 13:23, 28; cf. 12:2). This description reflects the Jewish custom *to recline* at the Passover. Yet, according to Josephus, the Essene custom was to dine while *sitting* (*J.W.* 2:130). The archaeological finds from Khirbet Qumran confirm Josephus' testimony that the Essenes did not recline but sat at their meals. As such, all the Gospels agree that Jesus did not follow the Essene custom of *sitting* at the Last Supper.

Finally, the numerous dishes from Khirbet Qumran and the testimony of Josephus represent another distinction between the custom of the Qumran Congregation and Jesus at the Last Supper. Customarily, light meals consisted of vegetable stews or lentils served in a large common bowl and sopped with bread by those sharing the meal. The scrupulous concern by the Essenes for matters of ritual purity prevented the members of the Qumran Congregation from sharing a common dish. The large number of dishes found at Khirbet Qumran—sufficient for 200 people—is consistent with Josephus' description of their meals: "The cook sets before each one plate with a single course" (*J.W.* 2:130).

Jesus had no such scruples at the Last Supper. He used the act of dipping in a common dish to identify his betrayer. "He who has dipped his hand in the dish with me, will betray me" (Matt 26:23; Mark 14:20; cf. John 13:26). The Gospels also attest to a single, common cup for the ceremonial sanctification of the wine [the *Qiddush*]. "And he took a cup, and when he had given thanks he said, 'Take this, and divide among yourselves'" (Luke 22:17). Jesus' actions would have been forbidden in an Essene setting.

While Jesus shared the popular critique of the first-century Sadducean priestly dynasty—the House of Hanin (Luke 3:2; Acts 4:6; *b. Pesah.* 57a; *t. Men.* 13:21)—he gives no hint that he shared the Essene rejection of the sanctity of the temple service. His followers continued to frequent the temple, also after the Cross (Luke 24:53; Acts 2:46). Even the Apostle Paul had no qualms about submitting to ritual immersion and ascending to the temple to offer sacrifices (Acts 21:17–26). These are hardly actions by a movement that saw the temple as spiritually obsolete or defiled.

## THE MYTH OF AN ESSENE QUARTER

One of the challenges for those who assume Jesus embraced the Qumran solar calendar has been to find an Essene setting in Jerusalem for the Last Supper, which brings us to the myth of an Essene quarter on Mount Zion. The line of reasoning linking a putative Essene Quarter and the setting for the Last Supper necessitates three assumptions. First, that there was in fact an Essene enclave on the southwestern hill of Jerusalem in the area today known as Mount Zion; second, that there is evidence of a continuity of Christian presence in the same area; and, finally, that this Christian presence memorialized the place of Jesus' Last Supper at or near the site of the presumed Essene Quarter in Jerusalem. We turn our attention now to the evidence for these assumptions.

The evidence falls into two categories: archaeological and literary. Simply stated, there exists today not a single piece of *archaeological* evidence that an Essene Quarter existed in Jerusalem in Jesus' day. Much of the recent conjecture is founded upon F. J. Bliss and A. C. Dickie's excavation in 1895 of a gate on the southwestern edge of the western hill of Jerusalem. Its Roman period level may indeed be the gate mentioned by Josephus in his description of the line of the first wall.

> Beginning at the same point [i.e., Hippicus Tower] in the other direction, westward, [the wall] descended past the place called *Bethso* to the Gate of the Essenes, then turned southwards above the fountain of Siloam; thence it again inclined to the east towards Solomon's pool, and after passing a spot which they call Ophlas [i.e., the Ophel], finally joined the eastern portico of the temple. (*J.W.* 5:145)

Notwithstanding Bliss's identification of the Gate of the Essenes, it is not necessary that this

## THE PROPOSED ESSENE QUARTER IN HERODIAN JERUSALEM

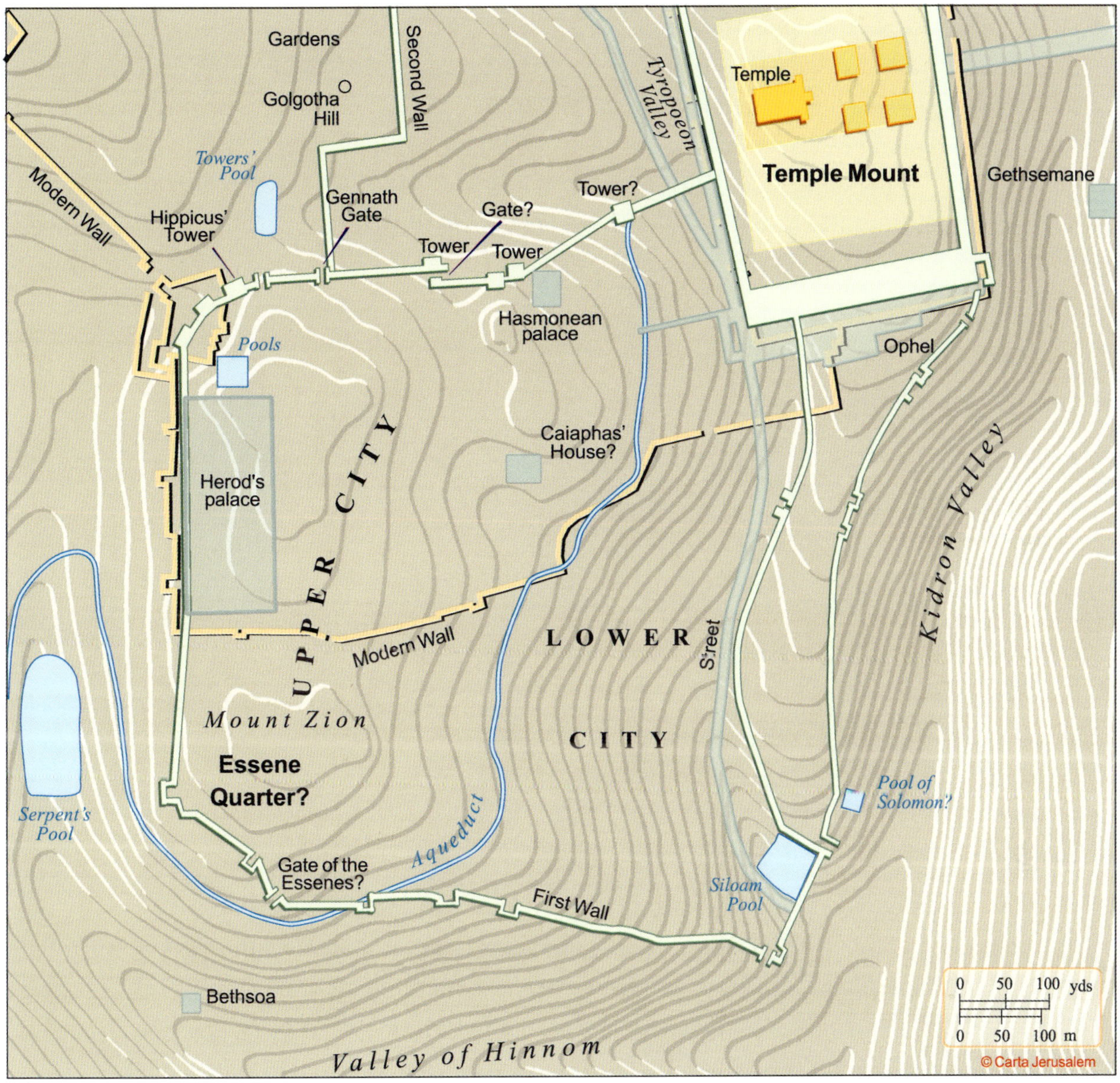


gate was named after an Essene Quarter within the walls of the city. If we follow the nomenclature of other gates in Herodian Jerusalem, it seems more likely that the epithet "Gate of the Essenes" indicated that the gate led to an Essene settlement *outside* of Jerusalem. The Gate of the Essenes led to a path that descended into the Hinnom Valley where it branched in two directions: one following the Hinnom into the Kidron Valley and the region of the Dead Sea and nearby Khirbet Qumran; the other followed the southern portions of the historic watershed route past Bethlehem to Hebron. We have no information how the Gate of the Essenes acquired its name. Lacking further evidence, there is no compelling reason to assume that the Gate of the Essenes signified an Essene Quarter within the walled city of Jerusalem.

Apart from the "Essene Gate," the only physical evidence proponents of an Essene Quarter can point to are ritual baths (*miqva'ot*) discovered in the vicinity of the gate. They see particular importance in the style of the *miqva'ot* with the parapet dividing the stairs leading into the baths. While

*Close-up view of the so-called Gate of the Essenes on Mount Zion showing the angle of looking into the city through the gate.* (photo Paul H. Wright)

ritual baths at Qumran do have this feature, they are routinely found with *miqva'ot* used by others. It is mistaken to assume that the parapet in the *miqva'ot* on Mount Zion necessitates that they belonged to an Essene community. The parapet was a common feature in ritual baths to prevent physical contact between the ritually defiled person entering the *miqveh* and the newly purified person leaving (cf. *m. Mid.* 2:2; *Let. Aris.* 160).

This feature can even be seen among the numerous *miqva'ot* excavated south of the southern wall of the Temple Mount. These baths were intended for Jewish pilgrims to purify themselves before entering the temple precincts (e.g., Acts 21:26; *P. Oxy.* 840). As we have already noted, according to Josephus and the Dead Sea Scrolls, the Essenes ceased active participation in the temple service (*Ant.* 18:19). The ritual baths near the entrance to the temple courts intended for purification and participation in the temple service have nothing to do with the Essenes. Thus, the parapet in the *miqva'ot* on Mount Zion provides no indication of who used these baths.

Further, excavations on Mount Zion in 1971–1972 led by Magen Broshi provide additional clear evidence that those living at the time on Mount Zion were not Essenes. Those who have assumed an Essene Quarter on Mount Zion have based their opinion upon Roland de Vaux's old chronology of Khirbet Qumran. They deem Broshi's identification of destruction from the earthquake on Mount Zion in 31 B.C. to be evidence for the beginning of an Essene settlement in Jerusalem. According to the theory the Essenes abandoned Khirbet Qumran and rebuilt the recently destroyed homes on Mount Zion during the reign of Herod the Great. Yet, if Jodi Magness's reassessment is correct and Khirbet Qumran was not abandoned after the earthquake, then the destruction and rebuilding of houses on Mount Zion in 31 B.C. have nothing to do with the question of whether or when an Essene Quarter was established on Mount Zion.

More importantly for our question is the remarkable nature of Broshi's finds among the rebuilt homes on Mount Zion. The excavators were surprised to find finely preserved frescoes from the period that contained motifs of birds and animals against floral backgrounds. Contemporary frescoes found at Masada, Jericho, Samaria and Caesarea possessed only geometrical shapes and imitations of colored marble. It seems that those who lived in these wealthy homes of the Upper City were remarkably lax concerning the prohibitions against depicted images of living creatures. From everything that we know about the Essenes, it is difficult to imagine even the most broad-minded Essene allowing such ornamentation to their decorated homes in the putative Essene Quarter on Mount Zion in Jerusalem. Moreover, what we know of Essene ideology, they willingly abandoned the pursuit of wealth and embraced a life of poverty. The richly adorned homes on first-century Mount Zion hardly reflect a life of poverty.

Josephus only mentions an Essene presence in Jerusalem in his report regarding Judah the Essene (*Ant.* 13:311–313), during the brief reign of Judah Aristobulus (104–103 B.C.). The date of Judah the Essene coincides approximately with the beginning of settlement at Khirbet Qumran. Whether Josephus' subsequent silence on the Essenes in Jerusalem and the ensuing occupation at Khirbet Qumran are related is beyond the scope of this work. We note the historian's silence because much is made of the story of another Essene, Menachem (*Ant.* 15:373–379) with the suggestion that this later episode marks the return of the Essenes to Jerusalem during the reign of Herod the Great.

Menachem first encountered Herod when the future king was still a young boy, and prophesied of his future reign. When Herod in fact became king, he called Menachem and asked him how long he would reign. The Essene predicted twenty or even thirty years, but he did not set a limit. This pleased Herod, and Josephus reports that, "from that time on he continued to hold all Essenes in honor" (*Ant.* 15:378). This story, like that of Judah, is intended only to illustrate the Essenes' renowned gift of prophecy, not to locate their residence (cf. Simon: *J.W.* 2:111–113). What is sometimes assumed by some modern readers but nowhere stated in the story about Menachem is that he was located in Jerusalem. We do not know where these events took place. Nor is there the slightest hint that Herod's esteem for the Essenes translated into the establishment of an Essene Quarter adjacent to his Jerusalem palace.

We return now to Josephus' reference to *Bethso* in the passage cited earlier in which he mentioned the Gate of the Essenes. *Bethso* has been associated by some with the instructions in the Temple Scroll intended for the Congregation living in eschatological Jerusalem.

> You are to build them a precinct for latrines outside the city. They shall go out there, on the northwest of the city: roofed outhouses with pits inside, into which the excrement will descend so as not to be visible. The outhouses must be three thousand cubits from any part of the city. (11QTemple 46:13–16; cf. 1QM 7:7; 4Q491 f1–3:7)

It is true that the direction of the latrines in the Temple Scroll northwest of the eschatological city is in the general direction of Josephus' *Bethso* near the Hippicus Tower. Even before the discovery of the Dead Sea Scrolls, Josephus' enigmatic term was thought to represent *beit tzo* (latrine). Nevertheless, the portrayal of latrines northwest of eschatological Jerusalem—even if this is the meaning for *Bethso* near the Hippicus Tower—is not evidence for an Essene Quarter on Mount Zion. The description of the Essene latrines in the Temple Scroll is not near Mount Zion, and Josephus makes no connection between *Bethso* and the Essenes. In addition, Yigael Yadin is correct that the philological relationship claimed by some between *shaveh* in the Copper Scroll (3Q15: 8:10, 14) and Josephus' *Bethso* is at best tenuous. In the end, we are left with disparate passages whose relationship is in question and individually provide little tangible evidence for an Essene presence in first-century Jerusalem.

The next assumption is that of a continuing Christian presence on Mount Zion subsequent to the destruction of Jerusalem in A.D. 70. Hillel Geva concluded that the modern excavations of the Jewish Quarter and the western hill of Jerusalem failed to find any significant resettlement in these areas during the Roman period following the destruction of Jerusalem. Instead, what we possess are Byzantine traditions preserved by Eusebius and Epiphanius that Jewish Christians settled there.

Finally, regarding the third assumption, neither these two Byzantine witnesses nor the earliest pilgrimage testimonies in the fourth century A.D. of the Bordeaux Pilgrim (A.D. 333) or Egeria (A.D. 381) make any mention of Mount Zion as the place of the Last Supper. It is not until a fifth-century statement by Hesychius that we hear this idea. Contrary to the often-heard suggestion, the preceding centuries of silence in Christian tradition are not the result of a "vow of silence" by the Gentile church, purportedly because these areas were still in the hands of Jewish Christians. Instead, the change in tradition in the fifth century A.D. is a direct result of the inherent ambiguity caused by the Latin translation of the New Testament.

Beginning with the Latin translations of the New Testament (A.D. 405), the different Greek terms for the place of the Last Supper (*anagion*: Mark 14:15; Luke 22:12) and the place where the disciples gathered after the Ascension (*hyperoon*: Acts 1:13) were rendered by the same Latin term, *cenaculum*. Can it be a coincidence that precisely at this time Christian tradition began to transfer the traditional site identification (which had previously been associated *only* with the gathering of the Apostles described in Acts), now also to the event of the Last Supper?

Whatever its cause, the fifth-century confusion regarding the location of the Last Supper on Mount Zion is not evidence of a previous Essene Quarter in the vicinity. Nor does it provide any support for the modern notion that Jesus ate his last meal according to the custom of the Essenes. The picture presented by modern archaeology and a careful reading of the ancient sources including the New Testament is consistent. There is nothing in the material or historical record to suggest that Jesus abandoned the Jerusalem temple to share in an Essene meal. Nor is there any evidence of an Essene Quarter on the western hill of Mount Zion in his day.

## CHAPTER 7

# The Lower City

Josephus introduces the designation "lower city" for the eastern hill of Jerusalem in his account of the Israelites' conquest of the Canaanite city (*Ant.* 5:123–124). Following the death of Adoni-bezek,

> [The Israelites] overran the district, taking the towns, and after capturing very many of them laid siege to Jerusalem. The lower city they mastered in time and slew all the inhabitants; but the upper city proved too difficult, through the strength of its walls, and the nature of the place. (*Ant.* 5:124)

As we have already noted, the historian confusedly assumed that the Jebusite city that David conquered and resettled was on the higher western hill (cf. *J.W.* 5:137). Thus, also on this occasion he assumes that the upper city of Jerusalem on the western hill existed as part of the Canaanite city. His presentation that the lower city fell, while the upper city resisted the Israelite siege, apparently was intended to reconcile the varying biblical accounts.

According to Judges 1:8, the Israelites took Jerusalem; "they put the city to the sword and set it on fire." However, a few verses later we are told, "The Benjamites, however, failed to dislodge the Jebusites, who were living in Jerusalem; to this day the Jebusites live there with the Benjamites" (Judg 1:21). An identical caveat is presented in Joshua 15:63, except that Benjamin is replaced with Judah. In order to reconcile the biblical description of the destruction of Jerusalem with its inhabitants and the subsequent presentation of the Israelites' inability to dislodge the Jebusites from their city, Josephus distinguished between the upper and the lower city. The former remained inviolable, while the lower city was conquered. It is also this lower hill that Josephus later designates with the Greek term *akra*: "The second hill, which bore the name Akra, and supported the lower city, is in the shape of a moon when it is horned" (*J.W.* 5:137).

## ANTONIA FORTRESS

Even a casual comparison between the earlier Hasmonean Palace and Herod's Royal Palace in the upper city of Jerusalem illustrates Herod's penchant for security. The three massive towers that guarded the entrance to his new residence were a product of the Idumean's legendary paranoia—a facet of his character that often had murderous consequences. Having deposed the ruling dynastic family of Hasmonean priests, Herod feared his greatest threat would come from the hierocratic elements of the Jewish population. So, it is no surprise that one of his first projects was to strengthen the fortress that overlooked the temple in order to maintain control of Jerusalem's sanctuary.

## POMPEY'S SIEGE OF JERUSALEM 63 B.C.

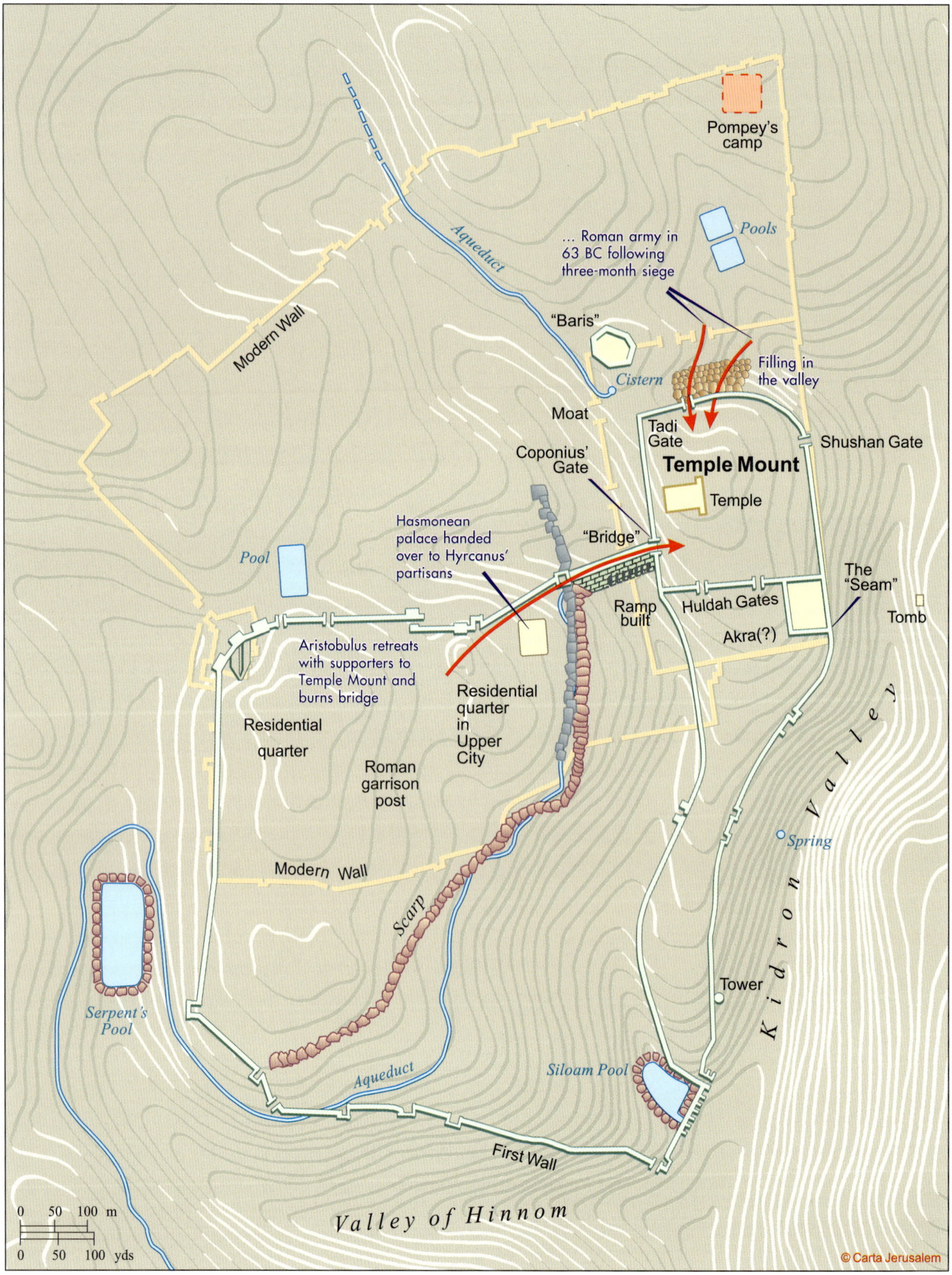


"Herod, the king of the Jews, made the Baris stronger to secure and guard the temple, and to gratify Antony, who was his friend and at the same time ruler of the Romans, he called it Antonia" (*Ant.*

15:409). "For if the temple lay as a fortress over the city, Antonia dominated the temple, and the occupants of that post were guards of all three" (*J.W.* 5:245).

Mark Antony had presented Herod to the Roman Senate and proposed that the Idumean be awarded the throne in Judea (*Ant.* 14:385; cf. App. *Bell. civ.* 5:75). The new monarch repaid Antony's support with the eponymous honor of his new construction. Most of Herod's major building projects occurred during a period of political and domestic tranquility from 25 to 13 B.C., but dedication of the Antonia must have occurred earlier. The Battle of Actium in 31 B.C. (Suet. *Aug.* 17:1–5) brought a dramatic shift in power in Rome. Octavian defeated Antony, and Herod's early supporter took his own life shortly afterwards in Egypt.

In a deft political maneuver, Herod embarked to Rhodes to swear allegiance to the new emperor, who now bore the title Caesar Augustus (*Ant.* 15:187–193). On that occasion Herod did not apologize for his previous friendship and support of Antony, but instead pledged to transfer the same loyalty to Augustus, if the new emperor would allow him. True to his promise, Herod honored Augustus with temples and cities across his kingdom, but in the same unapologetic manner, he never rescinded the honorific title given to the Antonia Fortress, named for his earlier benefactor and rival for Octavian's throne (cf. *J.W.* 1:118).

Our only literary description of the Antonia Fortress is that preserved by Josephus. Yet, he presents the modern reader with a conflicting historical and architectural picture, which in the absence of corroborating archaeological information limits our understanding of the fortress's origin and design. The relationship between the Antonia Fortress and the Baris, the earlier Hasmonean fortress, remains in question. "At an angle on the north side there had been built a citadel, well fortified and of unusual strength. It was the kings and high priests of the Hasmonean family before Herod who had built it and called it the Baris" (*Ant.* 15:403). "This was a fortress *near* the north side of the temple [precincts], which, as I said (cf. *J.W.* 1:75), was formerly called Baris, but afterwards took this new name under Antony's supremacy; just as Augustus and Agrippa gave their names to the cities of Sebaste and Agrippias" (*J.W.* 1:118).

Josephus seemingly attributes the construction of the Baris to the Hasmoneans, but as we have noted above (p. 16) there are historical references to a fortress by the same name near the temple already from the days of Nehemiah (Neh 2:8; 7:2). References to fortifications near the temple continue in the pre-Hasmonean works of the Letter of Aristeas (Let. Aris. 100) and Sirach (Sir 50:4). So, whatever Josephus meant by his statement that the Hasmoneans built the Baris, there is little question the fortress predates this family of priests and kings.

Further, the location of the Baris is a matter of scholarly debate. The English versions of Josephus' works routinely translate him to portray the Baris "adjoined, attached" to the Hasmonean square precinct surrounding the temple (*J.W.* 1:118). However, the Greek verb *proskesthai* means here "to lie near" and not "to adjoin," as it also does when Josephus describes the geographical proximity of the regions of Galilee and Judea in *Antiquities* 13:50. The borders of these regions are relatively "close," but they never touch.

Although the distance between the Baris and the walls surrounding the Hasmonean temple precincts was not great, it seems their separation was sufficient to explain the lack of any mention of the Baris in Pompey's siege of the temple precincts in 63 B.C. Instead, the Roman general's efforts were focused on Judah Aristobulus II and his supporters who had, "retired into the temple, cut the bridge which connected it with the city, and prepared to hold out to the last" (*J.W.* 1:143).

> Pompey himself was on the north side, engaged in banking up the fosse and the whole of the ravine with materials collected by the troops. The ravine once filled up, he erected lofty towers on the earthworks, brought up the battering engines which had been conveyed from Tyre, and tried their effect upon the walls.... However, the towers, which in this sector were extraordinarily massive and beautiful, long resisted the blows. (*J.W.* 1:145–147)

The error in rendering *The Jewish War* 1:118 to read that the Baris adjoined the temple has contributed to an unfortunate series of miscalculations concerning the location of both the Baris and the Antonia. It has led some to mistakenly conclude that the Baris and its initial Herodian replacement adjoined the Hasmonean walls of the temple, and so were *south* of the ravine described in Pompey's siege (see also Strabo, *Geog.* 16:40). The problem is that the historian subsequently describes the Antonia *north* of Herod's expanded precincts, and so *north* of the ravine after the depression was filled in as a part of Herod's renovations (*J.W.* 1:401; 5:238–247). Moreover, recent excavations in a tunnel along the western wall of the Temple Mount have unearthed foundation channels and cisterns that Dan Bahat identifies belonged to the Hasmonean Baris. Importantly, they were found north of the ravine mentioned above.

Nevertheless, to resolve what he mistakenly thought to be a contradiction in Josephus' testimony regarding the Baris and the Antonia, Leen Ritmeyer recently followed the nineteenth-century explorer Charles Warren's theory of two fortresses, both called Antonia. According to their solution, soon after the beginning of his rule, Herod rebuilt the Baris (possibly destroyed during Pompey's siege twenty-five years prior) and renamed it for Mark Antony. They surmise that both of these fortifications adjoined the walls of the Hasmonean temple precincts. Fifteen years later, when the Judean king extended the precincts northward, his earlier efforts were dismantled and a new fortress was built on the higher outcropping of rock upon which today is located at the 'Umariyyeh School. It is this second Herodian fortress that was personally known by Josephus.

Yet, as we have demonstrated, Warren and Ritmeyer's creative solution is unnecessary, and in fact stands at odds with the new archaeological evidence from the western wall tunnel. The modern confusion about the location of the Baris stems primarily from an error in translation, but Josephus has also contributed to the confusion with his well-documented penchant to employ toponyms anachronistically. Elsewhere, for example, he calls the Hellenistic city Pegae by its Herodian name Antipatris, while speaking of events during the earlier Hasmonean period (*J.W.* 1:99; *Ant.* 13:390). Yet, it is only *after* Herod assumed the throne that he renamed the city in honor of his father Antipater (*J.W.* 1:417; *Ant.* 16:143). In the case of the Baris and the Antonia, on several occasions Josephus employs the Herodian name (Antonia) to speak of the Baris in the pre-Herodian period (*Ant.* 13:307; *J.W.* 1:75, 118, 121).

We now have a better understanding of Josephus' description of the fortifications on the Temple Mount: (1) the Baris was "near" to the Hasmonean walled temple precincts but was not attached to them; (2) nothing in Josephus' testimony indicates the Baris lay south of the ravine mentioned in Pompey's siege that coursed near the Hasmonean temple precincts; (3) instead, the Baris was situated north of the ravine. Recent archaeological evidence confirms this reading of Josephus; (4) the distance of the Baris from the Hasmonean temple may explain its absence from the description of Pompey's siege; (5) the Baris was renamed Antonia in honor of Herod's early benefactor Mark Antony; (6) our reading of the Greek verb *proskesthai* to describe the location of the Baris and its Herodian replacement eliminates any need for "two Antonias"; (7) the location of the Antonia after Herod's renovations lay near the location of its earlier pre-expansionary location and that of its predecessor, the Hasmonean Baris. All were in the vicinity of today's 'Umariyyeh School in the modern Old City of Jerusalem.

**HERODIUM—PLAN OF THE PALACE-FORTRESS**

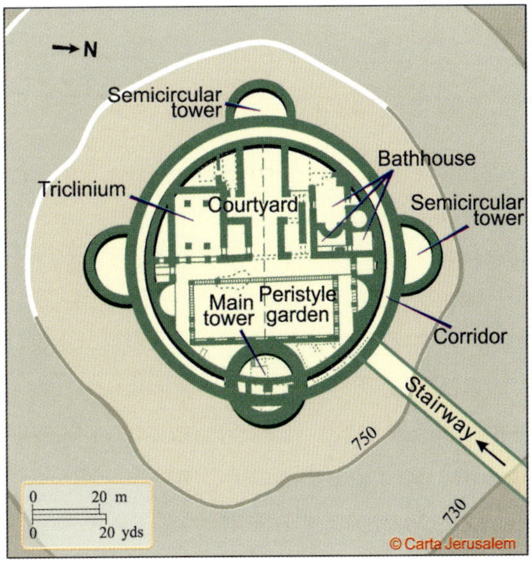


Little is left from the remains of the Antonia Fortress. Instead, we have only Josephus' historical description. The foundation for the fortress was a rocky escarpment 75 feet (25 m) in height (*J.W.* 5:238). This outcropping can still be seen on the northern edge of the precincts to the Muslim sanctuary. North of the citadel Herod's builders cut a deep moat in which was a pool called Struthion (*J.W.* 5:467), likely to be identified with the pool discovered under the convent of the Sisters of Zion at the Church of Ecce Homo. A century later Herod's impressive fortification would eventually fall, but for a time it did thwart the Roman advance during Titus' siege of Jerusalem in A.D. 70 (*J.W.* 5:467). It thus lived up to the historian's admiring depiction.

> To begin with, the [fifty cubit high] rock [upon which the fortress was built] was covered from its base upwards with smooth flagstones, both for ornament and in order that anyone attempting to ascend or descend it might slip off. Next in front of the actual edifice, there was a wall three cubits high; and behind this the tower of Antonia rose majestic to an altitude of forty cubits. The interior resembled a palace in it spaciousness and appointments, being divided into apartments of every description and for every purpose, including cloisters, baths and broad courtyards for the accommodation of troops; so that from its possession of all conveniences it seemed a town, from its magnificence a palace. The general appearance of the whole was that of a tower with other towers at each of the four corners; three of these turrets were fifty cubits high, while that at the south-east angle rose to seventy cubits, and so, commanded a view of the whole area of the temple. At the point where it impinged upon the porticoes of the temple, there were stairs leading down to both of them, by which the guards descended; for a Roman cohort was permanently quartered there. (*J.W.* 5:240–244)

To best grasp Josephus' portrait of the Antonia, the reader must compare it with other Herodian fortifications in Judea and parallels elsewhere in the Greco-Roman world. Ehud Netzer has noted that there are similarities in the design of the Antonia Fortress and the Herodium south of Bethlehem. Both were positioned on high sloping foundations and were comprised of four towers defending a central structure. Netzer has also drawn stylistic parallels between the Herodium and the Antonia Fortress with other *tetrapyrgion* (four-tower) Hellenistic buildings, which typically possessed one tower taller than the others. This feature has been identified in archaeological excavations at Herodium, and it likewise corresponds to the literary description of the Antonia, "three of these turrets were fifty cubits high, while that at the south-east angle rose to seventy cubits" (*J.W.* 5:242).

The Antonia's close proximity to the Jerusalem temple made the two installations closely linked. Earlier the Hasmoneans had begun the practice of keeping their priestly vestments in the Baris

(*Ant.* 15:403; 18:91–92). Herod continued the custom as an added measure of control over the priestly custodians of Jerusalem's temple (*Ant.* 18:91; cf. 20:6). The two are coupled in Josephus' description of Herod's efforts on the eastern hill. "The colonnades Herod reconstructed from the foundations; the fortress he restored at a lavish cost in a style no way inferior to that of a palace, and called it Antonia in honour of Antony" (*J.W.* 1:401; cf. 5:149).

Situated on the northwest corner of the temple enclosure (*J.W.* 5:238), the Antonia provided access to the sanctuary through the adjoining monumental cloisters with which Herod surrounded the temple (*J.W.* 2:403; 6:165). It was likely here that the Evangelist Luke intended when he describes the Roman troops escorting Paul from the temple precincts (Acts 21:34; cf. *Ant.* 18:55). Indeed, the Evangelist's detailed depiction that Paul stopped and requested to speak to the crowd "standing on the steps" dovetails precisely with Josephus' description of a staircase leading from the Antonia to the temple precincts, "there were stairs leading to both [the northern and western porticoes surrounding the temple precincts], by which the guards descended" (*J.W.* 5:244).

## THE COURT OF THE ELDERS

Excavations south of the Temple Mount in the area of the biblical Ophel uncovered monumental stairs that led to two sets of gates. Below these gates and among the debris from the Roman destruction of Jerusalem, archaeologists found a fragment from a finely inscribed stone plaque with Hebrew letters and a well-fashioned frame. To their amazement, the excavators realized that the fragmented inscription fit with another that had been discovered in Jerusalem by the French scholar Louis Félicien de Saulcy in the nineteenth century. The two pieces joined to form the upper left-hand corner of an inscribed plaque, which belonged to a building that stood near the southern gates to the Herodian Temple Mount. Benjamin Mazar reconstructed the last word of the first line, "Elders," and suggested that the inscription refers to the Elders of the Sanhedrin, who presided in this courthouse during the days of the Second Temple.

*Two fragments of an inscription found near the steps leading to the southern gate of the Temple Mount. Part of the Hebrew word* zekenim *(elders) in the inscription may refer to the elders of the Sanhedrin who gathered at the site.*

East of the Triple Gate where the inscription was found archaeologists have identified a large building from the Herodian period. Below the monumental steps first-century pilgrims gathered as they prepared for their final ascent to the temple. With help from the fragmentary inscription Mazar ventured that the Herodian period building should be identified with the Court of the Elders that stood "at the gate of the Temple Mount."

> Three courts were there [in Jerusalem]: *one used to sit at the gate of the Temple Mount*, one used to sit at the gate of the Temple Court, and one used to sit in the Chamber of Hewn Stone. (*m. Sanh.* 11:2)

For readers of the New Testament, identification of these meeting places for "the Elders of the Sanhedrin" is important to identify where the Sanhedrin convened (cf. Acts 5:27, 34; 23:1–8). Although the full council was likely not present (cf. Luke 23:51), according to Luke 22:66 it was to the "*sanhedrion*" or *council chamber* that the Sadducean priests brought Jesus to be questioned. Our building presents one of the possible locations for that tragic episode.

## THE PALACE OF THE ROYAL FAMILY OF ADIABENE

Archaeologists have recently made a tentative claim that they have discovered the missing palace of a legendary family from first-century Jerusalem on the northwestern side of the City of David (formerly the Givati Parking Lot). The royal family of Adiabene, a semi-independent vassal kingdom of the Parthians, left an indelible mark on the social and physical landscape of the Holy City. Ancient sources record the charitable deeds and building projects, which they accomplished there. Members of the Adiabene family are also praised for their support of the Jewish rebels during the First Revolt against Rome.

Several of the ancient literary witnesses to the Adiabene family center upon their conversion to Judaism. Queen Helena converted first and is described by Josephus as being "brought over to their laws" (*Ant.* 20:17). When Helena's son, the crown prince Izates, heard of his mother's favorable experience he became zealous to follow her example. Yet, his mother and a Jewish merchant named Ananias, who was responsible for teaching the king's other wives to worship God according to Jewish tradition, convinced Izates not to be circumcised. Helena's concern was that their subjects would not understand the heir-to-the-throne's pursuit of a foreign religion. Ananias further reasoned that Izates could worship God without circumcision, if he had indeed committed himself to the Jewish faith, since his devotion counted more than the physical act of circumcision. Nonetheless, on one occasion a certain Galilean named Eleazar—who was extremely strict regard-

*Late 19th-century photograph of the Tomb of the Kings.* (Library of Congress)

ing Jewish law—took the opportunity of Ananias' absence to criticize the king on his failure to follow through on his intentions:

> In your ignorance, O king, you are guilty of the greatest offence against the law and thereby against God. For you ought not merely to read the law but also, even more, to do what is commanded in it. How long will you continue to be uncircumcised? If you have not yet read the law concerning this matter, read it now, so that you may know what an impiety it is that you commit. (*Ant.* 20:44–46)

Upon hearing this, Izates immediately called his physician to perform the rite.

The members of the royal family who converted are routinely depicted as consummate converts. King Monobazus II, Helena's other son, is said to have made all of the handles of the vessels used on the Day of Atonement out of gold (*m. Yoma* 3:10). Additionally, Queen Helena set a golden candlestick over the door of the sanctuary and had a golden tablet crafted on which was written the so-called "Test for the Unfaithful Wife" passage from Numbers 5:11–31. When her son Izates went off to war, Helena vowed to be a nazirite for seven years should her son return alive (*m. Nazir* 3:6). The completion of this vow required Helena to be present in Jerusalem and to offer proper sacrifices at the temple (*m. Nazir* 3:6; 4:4). During the First Jewish Revolt kinsmen of the Adiabenes, Monobazus and Cenedeus, were numbered among the most valiant of several Jewish casualties (*J.W.* 2:520). After Titus commanded his men to plunder and burn Jerusalem, relatives of Izates and others from the city petitioned the emperor Vespasian for a pledge of protection (*J.W.* 6:356).

Jerusalem also marked the final resting place of Helena, Izates, and, perhaps, Monobazus II. Izates reigned for twenty-four years, and after his death his mother Helena succumbed to her grief. Monobazus II had their bones transported to Jerusalem and, according to Josephus, buried under the three pyramids that the queen had erected north of the city (*Ant.* 20:92–96).

The location of the massive tomb was well known in antiquity. Yet, likely because of its scale and decoration the tomb was mistakenly identified by subsequent European travelers with the tombs of the ancient kings of Judea. After his investigation in 1838, Edward Robinson recognized this error and argued on the basis of the description by Josephus and earlier visitors to Jerusalem that it was, in fact, the tomb of the Adiabene family. He credited Richard Pococke—an eighteenth-century English traveler—with being the first among more recent visitors to identify the tomb with the burial place of Helena and her sons.

Today, little remains of the three pyramids that once adorned the tomb. The pyramid, a funerary memorial known as a *nefesh*, reflects Egyptian architectural influence on

*Sarcophagus of Queen Sadan, wrongly identified as the sarcophagus of Queen Helena of Adiabene.* (photo Jeffrey Garcia)

*Inscription on the side of the sarcophagus of Queen Sadan.* (photo Jeffrey Garcia)

monumental Jewish tombs in the Second Temple period. One can still see them on ancient tombs located in the Kidron Valley. Evidence of the Adiabene tomb's rolling stone enclosure—a rare feature in first-century tombs—is still visible, having also gained the attention of the second-century A.D. Greek geographer, Pausanias.

> The Hebrews have a grave, that of Helen, a native woman, in the city of Jerusalem, which the Roman Emperor razed to the ground. There is a contrivance in the grave whereby the door, which like all of the grave is of stone, does not open until the year brings back the same day and the same hour. Then the mechanism, unaided, opens the door, which, after a short interval, shuts itself. This happens at that time, but should you at any other try to open the door you cannot do so; force will not open it, but only break it down. (*Descr.* 8.16:5)

Remarkably, he compares the Adiabene tomb to the legendary burial monument of Mausolaus at Halicarnassus, which was considered one of the wonders of the world. The mechanism for the tomb's opening has long since been destroyed, and there is some question how it worked. In all probability it was powered by water.

During an excavation of the tomb in 1863, Louis Félicien de Saulcy discovered several limestone sarcophagi. One was inscribed with two lines that read, "*tzadah malchatha*" and "*tzadan malkathah*," which translates Sadah [or Sadan] the queen. Inside of the sarcophagus were the remains of a person wrapped in a gold embroidered shroud. In spite of the fact that Robinson had correctly identified the tomb as belonging to Queen Helena almost thirty years earlier, de Saulcy insisted that the sarcophagus belonged to the wife of a Judahite king, perhaps Jehoaddan, the wife of King Joash (2 Chr 25:1). He thus unwittingly perpetuated the misnomer "Tomb of the Kings" that continues to this day.

Due to the discovery of human remains, a controversy arose in Jerusalem, and de Saulcy was forced to end his excavations. Before returning home, however, he found a way to ship the sarcophagus and other finds to Paris from Jaffa's port. In Paris, the sarcophagus was stored in the Louvre. On display for a short time, it was placed in storage until 1982 when there was an exhibition commemorating the 100th year of de Saulcy's passing. More recently, the Louvre loaned the sarcophagus to the Israel Museum in order to accompany the reopening of the Museum's archaeological wing in July 2010.

Until recently, scholarly consensus held that the sarcophagus belonged to Queen Helena. However, Jeffrey García and I demonstrated that the sarcophagus could not have belonged to the famous Adiabene matriarch. In his remarkable tale of discovery de Saulcy recounted finding a sealed loculus in which the sarcophagus was hidden. When they opened the stone sarcophagus, they found the remains of a woman dressed in fine attire. The bones disintegrated almost instantly, because they were exposed to the air after almost two millennia. Nevertheless, a few bones remained, which were examined by a renowned forensic anthropologist. He determined that she was a woman who had died at a young age.

According to Josephus, Helena died in mourning over the death of her second son, Izates, who died at the age of 55 (*Ant.* 20:92). Even if she had given birth to her children at a relatively young age, Helena must have lived into her 70s. If so, she can hardly have been the "young woman" found in our sarcophagus. It seems that Sadah [or Sadan] is a previously unknown queen, perhaps the wife of either of Helena's sons—Izates or Monobazus II—who were likewise interred in the tomb. Grave robbers raided another nearby loculus in the tomb, likely Queen Helena's chamber, leaving little behind. Yet, an ornate lid from a missing sarcophagus is on display in the Louvre and may have belonged to Helena's sarcophagus. It was found alone in a chamber that was dedicated for someone of great importance.

Despite what ancient sources and archaeology have told us about the Adiabene family, the location of Queen Helena's palace has remained missing, perhaps, until now. To date, archaeologists Doron Ben Ami and Yana Tchekhanovets have been able to uncover only a portion of a monumental building. What has been uncovered indicates that the structure was part of a spacious architectural complex, which consisted of two main structures—a southern and a northern one. Of the southern structure, only the northeastern corner has been exposed. The eastern wall of this structure is comprised of roughly cut fieldstones, and measures 46 feet (14 m) long. This wall, which extends westward beyond the excavation area, rises to a height of 16 feet (5 m) and is about 5 feet (1.5 m) thick. What has been preserved of the northern wall rises to about the same height as its eastern counterpart and is about 1 meter thick.

Archaeologists have discovered evidence that the structure was divided into elongated rooms that were oriented northwest to southeast. The basement level of the building was supported by rows of large vaults made of smooth rectangular-cut limestone ashlars. The bases of these vaults were discovered *in situ* while the upper courses collapsed when the building was demolished sometime during the Roman destruction of Jerusalem in A.D. 70—a date which was confirmed by pottery and coins. Remains of colored frescoed panels that adorned this complex were scattered amidst heaps of debris, and large architectural fragments with floral patterns were uncovered in secondary usage. Ornately decorated column drums and capitals were later incorporated within the walls of this southern structure to form part of the foundation of a later peristyle Roman building.

Further evidence of its demolition in A.D. 70 is the appearance of escape passages in the lowest floor of the building. Such protective measures were a result of the Roman onslaught and have been found elsewhere. In the summer of 2011, the Israel Antiquities Authority announced the discovery of a drainage canal that followed the length of a stepped street connecting the Temple Mount with the Siloam Pool. The discovery of a five-branched menorah etching, oil lamps, cooking pots, coins and a Roman sword in its original scabbard led archaeologists to conclude that it was used by rebels during the First Revolt to hide from the Romans.

Even less has been exposed of the northern structure, and most of it extends beyond the excavation area. Jewish ritual baths (*miqva'ot*) were dug into the ground on its northern side, as well as a square collection basin that likely fed the pools. The walls of the pools were plastered with grey

*Excavations at the former Givati Parking Lot, showing the possible remains of the palace of the Adiabene family.* (photo Jeffrey Garcia)

plaster common to the period. The presence of these pools is not strange when we consider the close proximity of this location to the southern entrance of the Temple Mount.

The presence of the shattered stone vessels also signals a concern for ritual purity, since stone in the Second Temple period was thought not to be susceptible to impurities. Excavations in Jerusalem's Jewish Quarter after the Six-Day War revealed several large homes with private immersion pools and stone vessels. These spacious homes, which likely belonged to aristocratic priests and their families, formed part of an upper-class enclave within the ancient city.

A building with such impressive dimensions naturally raises questions about its function. Construction on this scale in the lower city and independent of the city's fortifications lacks parallel. Many of the buildings excavated in this area of the city that date to the Second Temple period appear to be residences, although none match the size and construction of this building. The remains of frescoes in various solid colors are similar to what has been found in other upscale residences, like Avigad's Palatial Mansion in the Jewish Quarter and Herod's northern palace at Masada.

The precise location of Queen Helena's palace home is lacking in the ancient sources, but Josephus does provide some topographical clues. In the days of the First Revolt, the historian describes the infighting that plagued the rebel leaders' attempts to combat the Roman legions. Jerusalem was divided into three. Eleazar son of Simon held the inner courts of the temple, John of Gischala controlled the Temple Mount's outer court as well as part of the lower city, and Simon ben Giora, with the largest army of the three, held the upper city and parts of the lower city (*J.W.* 5:248–257).

The limits of Simon's control in the lower city are depicted by two palatial landmarks that belonged to the royal family of Adiabene.

> Simon occupied the upper city and the great wall as far as the Kidron (Valley); and a portion of the ancient wall where it bent back to the east from Siloam and descended until the palace of Monobazus (II), king of Adiabene beyond the Euphrates. He held also the spring and the Akra, that is the lower city as far as the (palace) of Helena, mother of Monobazus. (*J.W.* 5:252–253)

Josephus uses both palaces to mark the northern line of Simon's occupation of the lower city, one on the east and the other on the west. The palace of King Monobazus II was located near the ancient wall that coursed (north)east from the pool of Siloam along the eastern slopes of the City of David. The palace of Queen Helena is described together with "the spring" and "the Akra." Routinely, when Josephus refers to "the spring" in Jerusalem, he has in mind the western opening at which the Gihon flows out from rocky escarpment on the slope of the City of David (e.g., *J.W.* 5:140–145).

For Josephus the Greek term *akra* (height, hilltop, citadel) has various designations in Jerusalem. He uses it earlier in his report about King David's conquest of the Jebusite city to mean the City of David (*Ant.* 7:65). Later, he borrows from First Maccabees 1:33, which uses the term to identify a Hellenistic fortress built near the temple (*Ant.* 12:252). In our passage concerning the palace of Helena, the historian qualifies the term to mean "the lower city" which would, of course, include the area of the City of David (*J.W.* 5:253). Since the historian seeks here to demarcate the northernmost point of the southern neighborhood held by Simon where it meets the Ophel under John's control, the geographical markers suggest Helena's palace was in the lower city between the Ophel and the western outlet for the Gihon spring where it begins its descent to the pool of Siloam. The current excavations of the former Givati Parking Lot fall within this approximate area.

Another reference to a palace, "built by Grapte, who was a relative of Izates, the king of Adiabene," is mentioned in an earlier account (*J.W.* 4:567). Simon had entered the city to try and end John's tyrannical control. The resulting skirmish forced many of John's men to flee from this palace. Considering that Josephus' larger context, namely, Eleazar's expulsion of John from the temple's inner courts, and Simon's eventual control of both the upper city and most of the lower city, the palace mentioned as belonging to Izates might well be identical with Helena's.

Helena's palace is mentioned elsewhere in the burning of Jerusalem as being in the middle of the Akra (*J.W.* 6:355)—again meaning simply the lower city (*J.W.* 5:137). Generally, the lower city's urban sprawl is thought to have included the Tyropoeon Valley as well as the lower slopes of the southwestern hill. Since both John and Simon vied for control of the lower city, the dividing line between them is not readily clear. Archaeologists are correct, however, that few known possibilities exist for such a massive structure in the area of the City of David, and the palace of Queen Helena may be the best candidate. Of course, the archaeologists' suggestions are by no means certain and must await further excavation results.

The significance of the royal family's presence in Jerusalem is not limited to the locations of their palaces. As converts, the Adiabene family provides a fascinating window into the social and religious dynamics that existed in the early Jewish and Christian communities. As noted earlier, Izates was counseled by Ananias not to be circumcised because what was important was his adherence to the Jewish faith. It was Eleazar, a Galilean, who later convinced Izates that he had transgressed the law by not having the rite performed.

The importance of this episode for readers of the New Testament is that it illustrates that the issues of Jewish and Gentile relations, circumcision, and conversion, which lay at the center of many of the Apostle Paul's writings, were part of a broader internal Jewish debate, and not one that posed Christianity against Judaism. Circumcision of adult males both here and in the New Testament was not merely a ceremonial act, but the final step of full conversion to Judaism. The significance of the rite is summed up in the words of the Apostle Paul, "Every man who is circumcised is bound to keep the whole law" (Gal 5:3).

The royal family of Adiabene is likewise remembered in Jewish literature for its benevolence to the needy in Judea. During the famine of A.D. 46 (Acts 11:28; cf. Suet. *Claud.* 18:2; Tacit. *Ann.* 12:43; Dio *Hist.* 40:11) Queen Helena visited Jerusalem. After seeing the severity of the famine, she sent her attendants to Alexandria and Cyprus to secure grain and figs for the hungry. Her sons followed her example. Josephus reports that Izates likewise sent a large sum of money during the famine (*Ant.* 20:49–53), and rabbinic tradition remembers his brother and successor, Monobazus II, who emptied the royal treasury to assist the needy during another famine. He was criticized by some in his kingdom for squandering the treasures accumulated by his ancestors. He responded, "My fathers stored up below and *I am storing up above*" (i.e., in heaven; b. *B. Bat.* 11a; *t. Pe'ah* 4:18; *y. Pe'ah* 1:1, 15b). The king's sentiment reflects Jewish piety heard in the instructions of Tobit to his son: "Do not turn your face away from anyone who is poor, and the face of God will not be turned away from you.... So you will be *laying up a good treasure* for yourself against the day of necessity" (Tob 4:7–10). His words also echo the exhortation of Jesus to generosity towards those in need:

> Do not *store up for yourselves treasures* on earth, where moth and rust destroy, and where thieves break in and steal. But *store up for yourselves treasures* in heaven, where moth and rust do not destroy, and where thieves do not break in and steal. (Matt 6:20–21)

The discovery of a palatial residence in the area of the City of David, which may be the palace of Queen Helena of Adiabene, is an opportunity for us to pause and revisit the complex world of ancient Jerusalem and its people. The conversion of the royal house of Adiabene, specifically that of Izates, brings fresh light on an intra-Jewish debate, which also lay at the heart of the shifting social makeup in the early Christian community; namely the influx of Gentile Christians into what had previously been a Jewish movement. These early Jewish followers of Jesus embraced the importance placed on charity (Acts 10:34–35), which was a signature feature in Second Temple Judaism, and which also was a central aspect of Jesus' teaching (cf. Matt 6:1–2). This concern for the material welfare of others was also on display with the Adiabene family when they responded to the plight of famine that fell on Judea's inhabitants.

Further excavations may help to determine with greater certainty whether this is in fact Queen Helena's palace. In the meantime, the excavations in the Givati Parking Lot have added to our knowledge of Jerusalem's landscape shortly before the destruction of the city and once again prompted us to gain a better understanding of its setting for early Judaism and Christianity in the closing days of the Second Temple.

## THE SYNAGOGUE OF THEODOTUS

Excavations along the southern tip of the ridge of the City of David, under the direction of Raymond Weill in the winter of 1913–14, unearthed a series of buildings and water installations

*The Theodotus inscription.* (photo Peter Wong)

organized around an early Roman period synagogue. Parts of the buildings had been systematically dismantled and placed in a nearby cistern. Among the ruins was a dedicatory inscription in Greek for a synagogue built by a hitherto unknown Jerusalem patrician, Theodotus son of Vettenus.

> Theodotus [son] of Vettenus, priest and president of the synagogue (*archisynagogos*), son of a [previous] president of the synagogue, grandson of a [previous] president of the synagogue, built the synagogue for reading of the Law and teaching the commandments, and also the hospice and rooms and water installations for accommodation of the needy guests from abroad, which [synagogue] was founded by his ancestors and elders and Simonides.

We know little about the benefactor, other than that he was a priest and seems to have followed after his father and grandfather in his position as the president of the synagogue (cf. *m. Sot.* 7:7; *t. Meg.* 4:21). Paleographers date the inscription to the reign of Herod the Great (37–4 B.C.). Its description of the founding of the synagogue two generations prior to Theodotus, suggests the synagogue's existence at least 150 years before the Roman destruction of Jerusalem in A.D. 70. The inscription is important for tracing the early history and development of synagogues in the post-biblical period. It serves as physical collaboration for testimony from the written sources to the existence of synagogues during the days of the Second Temple, throughout Judea and in cities of the Greco-Roman world where Jewish communities flourished.

The Jerusalem Talmud speaks of 480 synagogues in Jerusalem during the days of the Second Temple (*y. Meg.* 3,1,73d). While the Theodotus inscription cannot verify the accuracy of this large number, it does indicate that synagogues played an important role in Jewish life, even in the shadow of the temple. Scholars have drawn attention to the stated activity of the synagogue, "for reading of the Law and teaching the commandments." There is no mention of communal prayers. Indeed, we have no mention of organized communal prayer in synagogues in the land of Israel prior to the destruction of the temple. Instead, the activity in the synagogue during the days of the Second Temple, as presented also in the Theodotus inscription, was primarily the reading and study of the Scriptures (cf. Jos. *Ag. Ap.* 2:175; Philo *Mos.* 2:215–216; Acts 15:21). In addition, the installations attached to the synagogue of Theodotus served to accommodate Jewish pilgrims to Jerusalem, who had traveled from abroad to worship in the Temple.

CHAPTER 8

# WATER SYSTEMS

THROUGHOUT JERUSALEM'S HISTORY access to water has remained a paramount concern. Initial settlement on the lower slopes of the eastern hill was determined by the only reliable local source of water—the Gihon Spring. Recent excavations have demonstrated the Canaanites expended considerable effort to assure that the population could safely obtain water—even during times of hostility. Little changed with the early Israelite settlement of Jerusalem, during the monarchial period from Kings David to Hezekiah (1004–721 B.C.). However, the advancing threat of the Assyrian Sennacherib in the eighth century B.C. spurred Hezekiah to redirect the waters of the Gihon through a manmade channel inside the city walls.

Record of the king's efforts is preserved in the summary of Hezekiah's accomplishments, "he made the pool and the tunnel by which he brought water into the city" (2 Kgs 20:20). A later report by the Chronicler gives an even more detailed description of Hezekiah's project. "It was Hezekiah who blocked the upper outlet of the Gihon spring and channeled the water down to the west side of the City of David" (2 Chr 32:30). The work of the laborers was memorialized in a dedicatory inscription etched on a channel wall:

> [...] the tunnel [...] and this is the story of the tunnel while [...] the axes were against each other and while three cubits were left to cut? [...] the voice of a man [...] called to his counterpart, [for] there was ZADA in the rock, on the right [...] and on the day of the tunnel (being finished) the stonecutters struck, each man towards his counterpart, ax against ax and flowed water from the source to the pool for 1200 cubits, and 100? cubits was the height over the head of the stonecutters [...]

As the biblical report indicates, the channel coursed over 500 yards (457 m) beneath the City of David, and arrived at the southwestern end of the ridge ending at the Pool of Siloam. The additional fortification wall with which Hezekiah encompassed the western hill assured that the pool destined to collect the waters of the Gihon spring would be accessible to the population during the Assyrian siege. Equally important, "the upper outlet of the Gihon" and the new channel were hidden in order to prevent access to the city's attackers. Similar efforts are seen at other fortified cities of Israelite settlement (e.g., Beersheba, Gezer, Megiddo, Hazor).

In time it seems that the origins for the source of the Siloam Pool were all but forgotten. In Jewish literature of the Greco-Roman period, the Gihon spring finds only distant historical reference (cf. Eus. *Onom.* 72:22). Josephus mentions it just once, when he recounts the coronation of Solomon (*Ant.* 7:355; cf. 1 Kgs 1:38–48). On the other hand, he refers mistakenly eight times to Siloam not as a pool, but as a spring (*pege*), "Siloam…so we called that spring of sweet and abundant water" (*J.W.* 5:140; cf. 5:145, 410, 505).

By chance the Hasmonean and Herodian remains of the Pool of Siloam were discovered recently. In June 2004 municipal workers were replacing a sewage pipe in Jerusalem's lower City of David, when they uncovered two stone steps. A salvage dig led by Ronny Reich and Eli Shukron further revealed a series of steps that measured 225 feet (68.6 m) long. Thus far uncovered, the steps consist of three segments, each of five descending steps with intervening narrow landings. The actual size of the pool would have varied according to the level of the water. As the water rose, it inundated additional segments of steps.

Isaiah is the first to record the pool's Hebrew name with his reference to "the waters of Shiloah" (Isa 8:6). Centuries later Nehemiah describes the repairs to the pool in the Persian period. "And Shallum the son of Colhozeh…built the wall of the Pool of Shelah of the king's garden, as far as the stairs that go down from the City of David" (Neh 3:15). The archaeologists have yet to find evidence for the pool's early date. Instead, two stages have been identified. In the first, the pool was plastered. Coins from the time of Alexander Jannaeus (103–76 B.C.) that were imbedded in the plaster suggest this work was completed at the end of the Hasmonean or beginning of the Herodian period. The plastering was later faced with the cut stone that is visible today.

While Josephus describes the pool as a source of drinking (cf. Luke 22:10), Reich and Shukron suggest its waters likewise were suitable to serve as a *miqveh*, a Jewish ritual immersion pool. Several questions must be answered before a sure conclusion can be drawn on this question. The New Testament account that mentions Siloam (John 9:1–11) does not bring us closer to an answer. The verb used in Jesus' instruction for the blind man "to wash" is never used to convey immersion, but instead the ritual washing of hands and face (*niptein*: Mark 7:3; John 13:5–14; 1 Tim 5:10). The Pool of Siloam did not need to be a ritual bath in order to serve the blind man of the Gospel account. Nevertheless, we have sufficient evidence to identify the newly found pool as the one to which Jesus directed the blind man in John 9:11, "Go to Siloam and wash."

*Hezekiah's Tunnel.*
(photo Zachary Wong)

*Remains of the Siloam Pool from the Second Temple period.* (photo Vladimir Neichin)

The expansion of Jerusalem during the Hasmonean period, especially during the reign of Alexander Jannaeus, meant the need for additional water resources beyond those provided by the Gihon spring. The so-called Lower Aqueduct was constructed at this time to bring water from ʻAin ʻAitan in the southern hills of Judea to the Temple Mount. Rabbinic literature describes this Lower Aqueduct, "The aqueduct led to [the temple] from Etam" (*y. Yoma* 41a; cf. *b. Yoma* 31a; *b. Zeb.* 54b). This may correspond to evidence of a dam dated to the Late Iron Age that served as a reservoir at this time.

It traveled from a massive reservoir called Solomon's Pools south of Bethlehem, at two points even tunneling under Bethlehem and the Jebel Mukabber ridge west of Government House south of the Old City of Jerusalem. Then it coursed along the southern slopes of today's Mount Zion. Remnants of the aqueduct can still be seen next to the steps leading from the Jewish Quarter to the Western Wall plaza. In the days of the Second Temple, the waters of the aqueduct were carried across the arched causeway that spanned the Tyropoeon Valley to a large cistern under the Temple Mount. During the First Jewish Revolt, this same aqueduct became a target of the insurgents, who were given the *nom de guerre* Sicarii (i.e., assassins), "The aqueduct which used to come from Etam, Sicarii once came and destroyed it" (*Lam. Rab.* 4:4).

Herod the Great directed water from Solomon's Pools also east to supply his desert fortress palace at Herodium.

> [Herod] built a fortress in the hills on the Arabian frontier sixty furlongs from Jerusalem…the crest he crowned with a ring of round towers; the enclosure was filled with gorgeous palaces…He had, at immense expense, an abundant supply of water brought into it from a distance… (*J.W.* 1:420)

He also built an upper aqueduct that directed waters to his Royal Palace in the area of today's Jaffa Gate of the Old City of Jerusalem.

**THE AQUEDUCTS TO JERUSALEM, SECOND TEMPLE PERIOD**

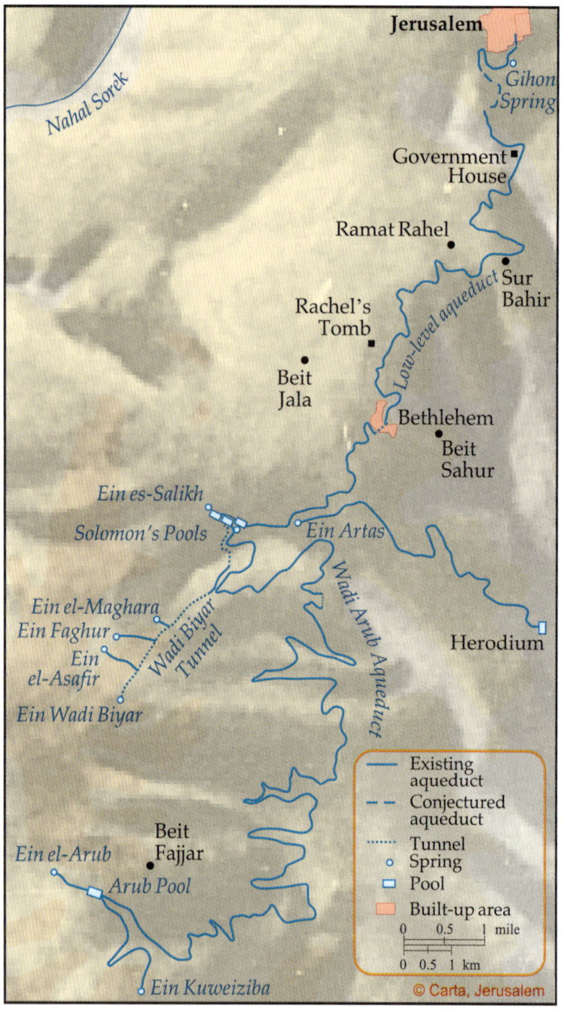


A recent survey has discovered another aqueduct in the environs of Jerusalem—one mentioned in an episode involving the prefect Pontius Pilate—which brought water from Ein el-Arub to Solomon's Pools.

> [Pilate] spent money from the sacred treasury (cf. *J.W.* 2:175–177: *qorbanas*; cf. *m. Sheq.* 3:2; Matt 27:6) in the construction of an aqueduct to bring water into Jerusalem, intercepting the source of the stream at a distance of 200 furlongs [twenty-three miles]. The Jews did not acquiesce in the operations that this involved; and tens of thousands of men assembled and cried out against him. (*Ant.* 18:60–62; cf. *Eccl. Hist.* 2.6.6–7)

Pilate's seizure of the temple treasury resembles other acts in which he demonstrated his contempt for local sensibilities (cf. *J.W.* 2:169–174; *Ant.* 18:55–59; Luke 13:1; Philo *Legat.* 299–306). The prefect's reckless disregard for local customs eventually led to his removal by the Romans (*Ant.* 18:85–89).

## RITUAL IMMERSION POOLS

Excavations in the area of the ancient Ophel along the Temple Mount's southern wall uncovered scores of Jewish ritual immersion pools (*miqva'ot*). Worshippers and pilgrims, who were required to purify themselves, utilized these pools before entering the precincts of the sanctuary. Many of the pools had a single entrance divided by a parapet. This low partition wall separated those entering for purification and those exiting.

Of special interest to the excavators, however, was a large immersion pool discovered below and to the east of the gates leading to the temple precincts. It differed from other ritual pools by its size. In addition, rather than possessing a single set of stairs to descend into the water, the basin was surrounded on all four sides by descending stairs. Unlike other nearby *miqva'ot*, this immersion pool had no partition wall on its steps to separate the suppliants.

The large immersion pool dates to the Herodian period, and its size suggests that it was intended for a great number of people. During festivals thousands of pilgrims could be expected to increase the already large crowds that frequented the temple for daily prayers and sacrifices. Ritual purity was an integral part of Jewish piety. Jewish law required that each *miqveh* be filled with at least 40 *seah*s of "living water" (*m. Miq.* 1:7; i.e., about 152 gallons [575 liters] of spring or rain water). Rock-hewn channels assured that water from nearby pools and cisterns flowed into the *miqva'ot*, especially during times of celebration.

The recent discovery of the ancient Pool of Siloam brought attention to the similarity of its design with this large ritual pool. There is little clear indication of a functional reason for their shared designs, other than serving public access. Meir Ben-Dov suggested that the large pool was intended exclusively for priests. Due to their responsibilities in the temple, it was important that they remained in a ready state of ritual purity. While it is likely that there were *miqva'ot* intended solely for use by priests, it remains uncertain that our large *miqveh* was limited to priests.

*The large immersion pool southeast of the Temple Mount.* (photo Marc Turnage)

## NORTHERN POOLS

The southward sloping topography of the eastern hill of Jerusalem contributed to the location of several collection pools north of the Temple Mount. Three pools lay in close proximity to Herod's renovations: the Pool of Israel, the Struthion Pool and the Pool of Bethesda. Their location was affected by a transversal valley that coursed south and east across the eastern hill, emptying into the larger Kidron Valley near the northeast corner of the Temple Mount.

Charles Warren investigated the Pool of Israel in 1869. He dated it to Herod's northern expansion of the temple precincts. The pool was constructed of large ashlars on three sides. The remaining western edge was cut into the bedrock, while the pool's monumental eastern wall served to dam the winter stream in the Beth Zetha Valley. As with the other pools in the vicinity, the functional relationship of the large 365-by-125-foot (110×38 m) collection pool to the temple is unclear.

Josephus mentions a nearby pool adjacent to the Antonia Fortress in his description of the Roman earthworks during their siege of Jerusalem: "The embankments were immense. Of the first two, that at Antonia was thrown up by the Legio V Macedonia over against the middle of the pool called Struthion, the other by the Legio XII Fulminata about twenty cubits away" (*J.W.* 5:247). The historian's statement regarding the pool is the only first-century reference we have to the Struthion Pool. Renovations of the Sisters of Zion Convent at the end of the nineteenth century uncovered the pool. It apparently belonged to the northern moat of the Antonia Fortress, and its location disrupted a Hasmonean aqueduct that earlier supplied water to the Temple Mount.

The Pool of Bethesda is indicated once in John 5:2: "Now there is in Jerusalem by the Sheep Gate a pool, in Hebrew called Bethzatha, which has five porticoes" (RSV). Wording in the verse presents the reader with several challenges. The elliptical description, reading literally that the pool was "at/by the sheep" (*epi te probatike*) has left the modern reader to decide whether the reference to sheep (*probatike*) was intended to signify a "sheep *market*" (KJV) or "sheep *gate*" (NIV, RSV). The confusion resulted in later Christian readers even attributing the designation *probatike* to the pool itself.

*The double-vaulted Struthion Pool.* (photo Zachary Wong)

> Bezatha: A reservoir in Jerusalem, which is also called "the *probatike*," previously having five porticoes. Now there is shown in the same place twin pools, one of which is filled from the annual rains, while remarkably the water of the other appears to be reddened, a trace so they say, resulting from earlier submerging of the sacrifices in it. Consequently, it is also called "the *probatike*" [i.e., the Sheep *Pool*], because of the sacrifices.
>
> (Eus. *Onom.* 58:21–26)

Not only has the ambiguity of the Johannine passage resulted in a new Christian place name, the Sheep Pool, it also seems to have been the genesis for a legend that saw stains from the blood of sacrificial animals washed in the pool. All of this stems from the enigmatic reading of *probatike* in John 5:2. It seems far more probable that the mention of "the sheep" in our verse is related to a nearby fixture, a gate. Already in the days of Nehemiah, there was a gate in the vicinity called "the Sheep Gate" (Neh 3:1, 32; 12:39).

In addition, to determine the etymology of the pool's name, the modern reader must decide among its multiple, variant spellings in the manuscript witnesses. Some manuscripts read Bethsaida ($P^{66}$, $P^{75}$, Codex Vaticanus). Similarly, at the end of the fourth century Jerome replaced Eusebius' earlier toponym of Bezatha with Bethsaida (Latin *Onom.* 58:21). However, the appearance of Bethsaida in these witnesses is merely the consequence of the scribal penchant to exchange the known for the unknown. In this instance, the relatively unknown name of Bezatha has been abandoned for the better-known name of the Galilean fishing village in which Jesus also performed a healing (Mark 8:22–25).

The more likely spelling for the toponym is the variant Bethesda (NIV, KJV, ASV) or Bethzatha (RSV, NRSV). Scholars have attempted to trace the etymology of both of these names, based on

John's statement concerning its Hebraic character. The most common suggestion for the Hebrew origin of Bethesda is *beit ḥisda* (place of mercy) or *beth 'ašda* (place of pouring). The former proposal has some appeal because of the apparent tradition regarding divine mercy exhibited in healings at the pool, but the philological argument for *beit ḥisda* as an equivalent for *bethesda* is not persuasive.

The proposal of *beth 'ašda* has gained more recent support because of a line from the Qumran Copper Scroll (3Q15) in which mention is made of a pool in Jerusalem. Geza Vermes renders the relevant line: "Next to them, at Beth-Eshdatain (Bethesda), in the reservoir where you enter the small pool…" (3Q15 11:10). However, more recent scholarship has abandoned this Hebrew reconstruction and no longer reads the Hebrew word to be Beth-Eshdatain but a common plural noun, "reservoirs" (*ʾʾśwḥyn*). If this reconstruction is correct, then the expression from the Copper Scroll no longer has a bearing on Bethesda or its etymology.

As we have noted, the spelling Bethzatha resembles Eusebius' Bezatha in his pre-Byzantine Greek *Onomasticon* (c. A.D. 305). It is also found in the New Testament manuscript, Codex Sinaiticus. Variants of this form may be preserved in Codex Bezae and western manuscripts (*Betzetha*), and some Latin versions (*Bezatha*). Of added significance is the report by Josephus that the new, northern suburbs of Jerusalem walled in by King Agrippa I—which included the area of the pool—were called Bezetha.

> This wall was built by Agrippa to enclose the later additions to the city, which were quite unprotected; for the town, overflowing with inhabitants, had gradually crept beyond the ramparts. Indeed, the population, uniting to the hill the district north of the temple, had encroached so far that even a fourth hill was surrounded with houses.

*Remains of the Pool of Bethesda, with the Church of St. Anne in background.* (photo Shmuel Magal)

> This hill, which is called Bezetha, lay opposite Antonia, but was cut off from it by a deep fosse…The recently built quarter was called in the vernacular Bezetha, which might be translated into Greek as New City [or more correctly as he reports in *J.W.* 2:530: "the district called Betheza *and also* New City]."
>
> (*J.W.* 5:148–151; *Ant.* 19:326; cf. *J.W.* 2:328; 5:246 [Bezatha])

The careful Greek reader will recognize that even in the various references by Josephus, the manuscripts present three close but different spellings for the newly enclosed suburbs (i.e., Bezetha, Bezatha, Betheza); yet the quarter described by Josephus in each variant is the same one that lay on the hill north of the Temple Mount, near the Antonia Fortress.

The neighborhood encompassed the area of the Pool of Bethzatha. For our purposes, what is important is to note that the name for the district closely resembles the New Testament name for the pool found in important manuscript witnesses. It seems that the name for the area for Agrippa's expansion to the walled city of Jerusalem was related to the name of the pools. While the precise etymology of Josephus' Bezetha or John's Bethzatha will likely remain uncertain, it may be that the neighborhood and the pool located in it derived their names from the local agriculture. Other examples of this custom exist in the environs of Jerusalem (e.g., Gennath Gate [Garden Gate], Mount of Olives, Bethphage [place of figs], etc.). If so, the toponym for the district and pools may have been derived from the Hebrew *beit-zayit* (place of olives).

Outside of John's Gospel and later Christian witnesses, we have no clear literary references to the Pool of Bezatha. Benjamin Mazar proposed that this pool is the one attributed to Simeon the Righteous in the second-century B.C. work of Ben Sira.

> The leader of his brothers and the pride of his people
> was the high priest, Simon son of Onias,
> who in his life repaired the house,
> and in his time fortified the temple.
> He laid the foundations for the high double walls,
> the high retaining walls for the temple enclosure.
> *In his days a water cistern was dug,*
> *a reservoir like the sea in circumference.* (Sir 50:1–3)

Unfortunately, excavations at the beginning of the twentieth century by the White Fathers, custodians of the site, failed to find archaeological evidence of the pool's existence during the days of Simeon in the early part of the second century B.C. Instead, excavators uncovered two adjoining pools from the early Roman period and fragmented columns that belonged to the pools' porticoes. Subsequent to Eusebius, the next mention of the pools is by the Bordeaux Pilgrim who visited Jerusalem in A.D. 333. He repeats much of Eusebius' earlier description of the twin pools (including Jerome's mistaken Bethsaida) and the local healing traditions attached to them.

> Farther in the city are twin pools (*piscinae gemellares*), having five porticoes, which are called Bethsaida (*Betsaida*). There those who have been sick for many years are cured. The pools contain water which is red when it is disturbed (*in modum coccini turbatam*). (*Itinerarium Burdigalense* 589.7)

The discovery of a marble foot with a Greek inscription in the excavations indicates that the object served as a votive offering, and further that the pools may have become a place of healing (i.e., an Asclepeion) also for pagans in the late Roman period.

CHAPTER 9

# Herod's Temple

The building projects of Herod in Judea are unrivaled. Yet, his efforts towards the expansion and improvements to the Jerusalem temple were the jewel in the crown of the king's considerable accomplishments. Even his detractors recorded in the Bablyonian Talmud had to concede, "He who has not seen the building of Herod, has not seen a beautiful building in his life" (*b. B. Batra* 3b; cf. Luke 21:5; Mark 13:1). Verifiable details concerning Herod's Temple are not yet possible. After a century of archaeological excavations in Jerusalem, no scientific investigation has ever been carried out within the Haram esh-Sharif, site of Solomon and Herod's Temples and today under the control of the Muslim Waqf. What evidence we can glean to sketch Herod's Temple is drawn from ancient literary witnesses, observations by nineteenth-century explorers and fragmentary modern evidence. The literary information is difficult because of inconsistencies between the descriptions of late biblical material (Ezekiel, Ezra, Nehemiah), Josephus, the New Testament and rabbinic literature.

Josephus reports that Herod initiated his work on the temple in the eighteenth year of his reign (20–19 B.C.). The main portion of the construction took nine-and-a-half years (*Ant.* 15:380–402), but work continued until it was fully completed during the procuratorship of Albinus in A.D. 62–64 (*Ant.* 20:219; cf. John 2:20). Indeed, recent finds by Reich and Shukron indicate that the section of the wall under Robinson's Arch on the southwest corner was only constructed in the first century A.D., some twenty years after Herod's death. Herod's efforts faced two challenges: expansion of the precincts that surrounded the sanctuary and improvements to the temple itself that had been built under Zerubbabel (Ezra 3:1–13). Herod was limited by the topography of the eastern hill. The ridge slopes southward towards the ancient City of David with severe faces on its eastern and western edges. To expand the courts surrounding the sanctuary Herod had to reshape the hill. To the northwest of the temple, he quarried away the rising bedrock and filled in a fosse that coursed across the northwest corner of the expanded precincts. On the westward and southern sides he constructed buttress walls behind which vaults supported the platform for the temple courts. His efforts were so successful that Herod was able to double the surface area around the sanctuary. The current walls of the Haram esh-Sharif retain Herod's expansion in a trapezoidal-shaped esplanade measuring 525 yards (480 m) on the west, 514 yards (470 m) on the east, 345 yards (315 m) on the north and 306 yards (280 m) on the south. The resulting area of the sanctuary is 172,220 square yards (144,000 sq. m) or over twice the area described in the Mishnah.

The Temple Mount measured five hundred cubits by five hundred cubits [c. 820 × 820 ft./250 × 250 m]. Its larg-

## PLAN OF THE HERODIAN TEMPLE COMPLEX

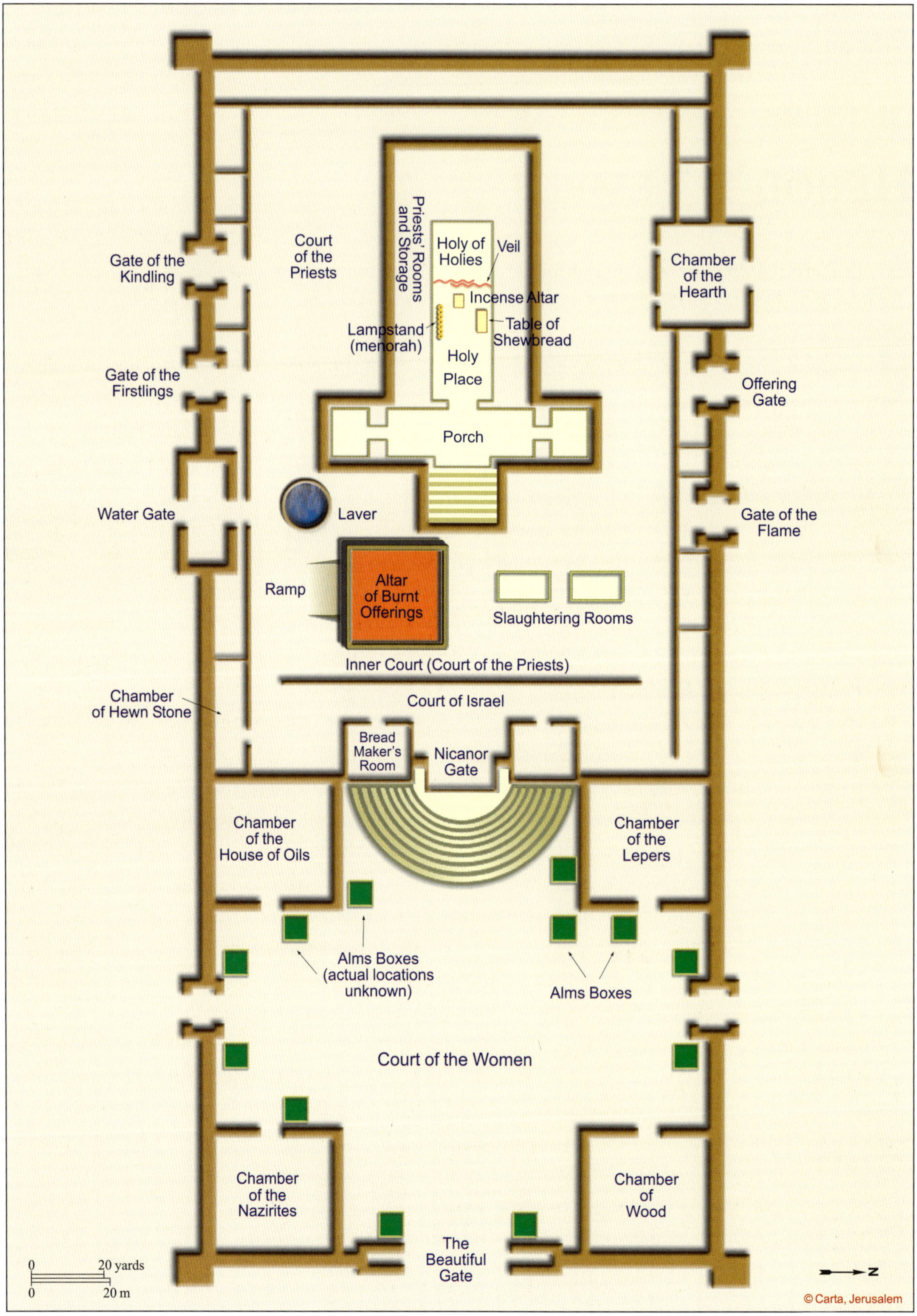

> est [open] space was to the south, the next largest to the east, the third largest to the north, and its smallest [open space] was to the west; the place where its measure was greatest was where its use was greatest. (*m. Mid.* 2:1)

The difference between the smaller dimensions given by Israel's Sages and Herod's sanctuary indicates that the rabbis did not attribute the same degree of sanctity to the area of Herod's expansion. If the current assumed location of the altar stood at the Dome of the Rock and was the center of the rabbinic measurement, then the eastern and western sides of the sacred space approximate the current Herodian walls. The variation between the two areas is primarily to the south and north, precisely the focus of Herod's expansionary efforts. Owing to the sharp decline on the mount's southeastern side, one can still see standing the greatest height in the wall at 148 feet (45 m). The scale of Herod's *temenos* was one of the largest in the Roman world, matched only by the Roman sanctuaries built later at Damascus and Palmyra.

*(above) Remains of the Roman sanctuaries built in the* temenos *style in Palmyra and (left) the Temple of Bel before its destruction by ISIS.*
(photos: R. Steven Notley)

# THE STONE INDUSTRY OF JERUSALEM

*Herodian stone jars and table discovered in the Jewish Quarter excavations.* (photo Zachary Wong)

A wide array of stone vessels and utensils were uncovered in excavations from first-century Jerusalem. Their numbers highlight the dramatic increase in the stone-carving industry centered in Jerusalem during the rule of the Herodians. Herod the Great initiated monumental building projects throughout the country. Skilled artisans were needed to complete his designs. With large numbers of stoneworkers available, it is no surprise to find an increase in objects created from the same limestone. Nowhere was the colossal scale of Herod's efforts on display more than in Jerusalem. The concentration of stone masons in the capital city likely contributed to Jerusalem's leading role in the stoneware industry.

Evolving purity laws in this period likewise reflect the increasing importance of Jerusalem's stone industry. The Sages deemed fired pottery susceptible to ritual uncleanness, while stone was not (cf. *m. Kelim* 10:1; *m. Ohal.* 5:5; *m. Parah* 5:5; *m. Yad.* 1:2). For the population of Jerusalem, where the city's economy revolved around the temple, issues of ritual purity touched on every facet of daily life. Consequently, these rabbinic opinions strengthened the importance of a Jerusalem-centered industry.

The discovery of large stone jars to store drinking water illustrates the extent of the people's concern for ritual purity. Before archaeologists unearthed them, the only ancient literary witness to such large stone storage vessels was John 2:6: "Now standing there were six stone water jars for the Jewish rites of purification, each holding twenty or thirty gallons." The New Testament passage aptly describes the size of the vessels, and likewise their purpose—to keep on hand ritually pure drinking water. The description in the Gospel of John tells us that the relatives of Jesus in Cana, like pious residents in Jerusalem, took to heart the contemporary precepts regarding ritual purity. Stone jars such as these correct the popular misperceptions about the Galilee—that its residents were not concerned with ritual purity and other matters of religious devotion. Instead, the archaeological record indicates little difference between Jerusalem and Galilee. In fact, in some instances the care by the population of Galilee concerning the commandments exceeded even those of Judea.

Another noteworthy innovation in Jewish custom during the Herodian period, which was also likely a product of Jerusalem's developing stone industry, was the change in the community's burial practices. In the preceding period, the body of the deceased was placed on a shelf in an enclosed family tomb and left for a year. On the anniversary of the burial, the tomb was reopened and the skeletal remains moved to a respository pit in the tomb where the bones of other deceased family members had been laid. This practice of secondary burial is what lies behind by the oft-repeated phrase in the Hebrew Bible that the dead were "gathered to their fathers" (e.g., Gen 49:29; Judg 2:10; 2 Kings 22:20, 2 Chr 34:28).

In the Herodian period the secondary burial of the deceased is frequently in stone ossuaries rather than in repositories. The stone receptacle for the deceased's bones was carved from the soft limestone quarries that surround Jerusalem. We have no explanation in the literary sources for this change in burial custom, and some scholars have theorized that it was related to advancing Jewish notions about the afterlife and belief in the resurrection. However, it seems more likely that this change was born not out of ideological motives, but the increased availability of masonry skills that allowed the loved ones to be honored with a more ornate style of burial. The practice of ossuary burials in Roman Judea lasted for about a century and the gradual abandonment of this style of interment coincided with the decline in building projects in Jerusalem—further indicating that the best explanation for Jewish ossuary burial was the flourishing stone industry in Second Temple Jerusalem.

*Ossuary of the high priest Caiaphas, found in Jerusalem in 1990 and now on display in The Israel Museum.* (photo Deror Avi, via Wikimedia Commons)

In December 1990 the oldest ossuary found to belong to a known historical figure was unearthed south of the Old City of Jerusalem. The family tomb was opened and one of the ossuaries was inscribed "Joseph son of Caiaphas." Josephus reports that in the first century Annas, father-in-law to Caiaphas (Luke 3:2; John 18:13, 24; Acts 4:6) was buried nearby to where the Caiaphas family tomb was discovered. The tomb of Annas served as a point of reference for the historian's description of Titus' siege wall around Jerusalem:

> [Titus] directed the wall toward the lower region of the New Town and from there across the Kidron to the Mount of Olives; then bending toward the south, it enclosed the mount as far as the rock called Peristereon and the adjoining hill which overhangs the Siloam ravine. From there, turning westward, the wall descended into the Valley of the Fountain, and then ascended to the burial monument of Ananus [Annas] the high priest.... (*J.W.* 504–505).

Scholars are in agreement that the ornate ossuary from this newly discovered tomb belongs to the high priest, Caiaphas—one of the primary figures mentioned in the events that led to Jesus' death. The discovery of an ossuary burial for such a prominent Sadducean priest—whose sect did not believe in the ressurection (Acts 23:8; *A.J.* 18:16)—further strengthens the suggestion that use of ossuaries in first-century Judea had little to do with belief in the afterlife.

## THE GATES

Access to the temple precincts was gained through gates built in the four buttress walls. The description and numbers of these differ between the Mishnaic tractate *Middot* and Josephus. In the Jewish historian's lengthy description of Herod's efforts (*Ant.* 15:380–423; *J.W.* 1:401–402), he only details gates on the west and south. When picturing the north, his focus is the Antonia Fortress; and on the east, Solomon's Portico. Various attempts have been made to try and reconcile the picture of Josephus and the rabbis. Complicating matters is a fact that we stated at the outset and should always be kept in mind when speaking about the Temple Mount. There has never been a scientific archaeological investigation of the site. Certainty remains, quite literally, out of reach.

We will proceed with the assumption that there is some measure of correspondence in the description of Josephus and the rabbinic sources. We do so recognizing that Leen Ritmeyer's recent novel proposal may be correct. He suggests that Mishnah *Middot* only describes the earlier pre-Herodian square-walled Temple Mount. After Herod's expansion, this previous Hasmonean wall with its gates was left as a type of walled inner enclosure. The difficulty with Ritmeyer's idea is that this inner wall receives no mention in Josephus' detailed description of the Temple Mount in his day. Did he inadvertently forget to mention it? Or was it not there?

If Ritmeyer is correct, then the gates named in the rabbinic sources do not correspond to the existing (and those no longer existing) Herodian gates that are visible today. For example, the external twin gates on the south may have provided entrance up to the inner, juxtaposed Huldah Gates. Likewise, the gate we have described below as Wilson's Gate (which no longer exists) may have provided access to an inner gate, which was called by the rabbis Coponius' Gate.

Our aim in proceeding is not to argue the unfailing certainty of the description that follows, but

*This 19th-century photograph of Cistern 1, on the Temple Mount, is the only indication above ground of the Tadi Gate.* (photo S. Narinsky)

more modestly to introduce the reader to the setting of the Temple Mount in the first century, in the period of the New Testament and the final days of the Second Temple.

## North: Tadi Gate

Only one gate from the north is mentioned in the rabbinic sources, "the Tadi Gate on the north, which was not used at all" (*m. Mid.* 1:3; cf. 1:9). The Mishnah also describes the gate's unique design, "All the gates that were there had lintels, save only the Tadi Gate over which two stones leaned the one against the other" (*m. Mid.* 2:3). Josephus only mentions in passing an unnamed "northern gate" in his account of Titus' siege of Jerusalem (*J.W.* 6:222).

The position of the northern approach was necessarily limited. On the eastern half of the wall, the descent of the Bezetha Valley made it unsuitable for a gate, while the Antonia dominated the western portion. As described above, beyond the walls of the temple enclosure lay the Antonia Fortress on its northwestern corner. Under the Hasmoneans and Herod the priestly robes were kept here.

> At the angle on the north side there had been built a citadel, well fortified and of unusual strength. It was the kings and high priests of the Hasmonean family before Herod who had built it and called it the Baris. Here they had deposited the priestly robe that the high priest put on only when he had to offer sacrifice. This robe Herod kept safe in that place, and after his death it was in the custody of the Romans until the time of Tiberius Caesar. (*Ant.* 15:403).

Custody of the priestly vestments later became a point of contention between the Jews and the

Romans who continued the custom (*Ant.* 15:406–409; cf. 18:90–95; Tac. *Ann.* 6:32). Rome likely sought custody of the robes in order to control the priestly establishment and its temple activities.

## East: Shushan Gate

In the description of Agrippa's completion of Herod's expansion of the *temenos*, sixty years after his great-grandfather's death, Josephus attributes the eastern outer wall of the sanctuary precincts to Solomon.

> They urged [Agrippa II] to raise the height of the east portico. This portico was part of the outer temple, and was situated in a deep ravine (i.e., the Kidron). It had walls four hundred cubits (c. 656 ft./200 m) long and was constructed of square stones, completely white, each stone being twenty cubits long and six high. This was the work of King Solomon, who was the first to build the whole temple. (*Ant.* 20:221; cf. *J.W.* 5:184)

Josephus' description of the earlier low height of the eastern wall is repeated by the tractate *Middot*, "All the walls there were high, save only the eastern wall, because the [High] Priest that burns the [Red] Heifer and stands on the top of the Mount of Olives should be able to look directly into the entrance of the Sanctuary when the blood is sprinkled" (*m. Mid.* 2:4; cf. *m. Parah* 4:2). The rabbinic description of the eastern wall suggests once again that its presentation lacks the Herodian innovations. Both the rabbinic report and Josephus' description prior to the renovations of Agrippa draw attention to the eastern wall being lower than the other three sides.

The New Testament (John 10:23; Acts 3:11; 5:12) and Josephus attribute the eastern wall to Solomon, but this claim is open to challenge. Nevertheless, it does suggest that its construction pre-dated the other porticoes, and that portions likely existed before Herod. There is evidence of pre-Herodian workmanship in the masonry of the wall. About 105 feet (32 m) north of the southeastern corner is a visible masonry seam that marks the line of Herod's extension for the Royal Stoa. South of the seam, the well-known Herodian masonry style is evident, with the flat boss and framed drafts. North of this line, a different style is seen with a protruding boss. There is scholarly discussion whether at least some of these stones were pre-Hasmonean and comprised the Seleucid Akra, were Hasmonean construction, or were earlier Herodian ef-

*The Seam along the eastern wall of the Temple Mount; on the right, Hellenistic and/or Hasmonean construction, on the left Herodian masonry* (photo Oren Rozen, via Wikimedia Commons)

forts before his expansion work that included the Royal Stoa.

While questions may exist regarding the beginnings of the eastern wall, there is no doubt that the present eastern gate, known as the Golden Gate (or in Arabic, the Mercy Gate), is of considerably later construction. It is conjectured by some that the current closed entrance lies above an earlier first-century one. This theory garnered support with the accidental discovery in 1981 of an earlier arched gate, whose date cannot be determined, immediately beneath the Golden Gate. Yet, some challenge remains. The ancient witnesses describe the lintel for the eastern gate having two stones, not an arched lintel as the one photographed beneath the current eastern gate. In any event, *Middot* informs us how the eastern Shushan Gate earned its name, "the Eastern Gate on which was portrayed the Palace of Shushan" (*m. Mid.* 1:8; cf. *m. Kelim* 17:9; *J.W.* 6:244; *b. Men.* 98a).

## West: The Four Gates

The description of the western entrance to the Temple Mount is the point of greatest variance in the ancient sources. Mishnah *Middot* speaks of a single gate, "the Coponius Gate on the west, that served for coming in and for going out" (*m. Mid.* 1:3). Josephus, on the other hand, describes four gates.

> In the western part of the court [of the temple] there were four gates. One led to the palace by a passage over the intervening ravine, two others led to the suburbs, and the last to the other part of the city, from which it was separated by many steps going down to the ravine from here up again to the hill. (*Ant.* 15:410)

Modern archaeology has confirmed Josephus' depiction. Yet, the modern reader may be confused, because the historian does not present the gates in order. In the first century there existed two of each, alternating lower and upper gates. Today they are called by the names of the modern explorers who rediscovered them. From north to south, the first lower gate opened onto a Herodian thoroughfare that led to the northern suburbs of Bezetha. The British explorer, Charles Warren, found the gate and it is still popularly called by his name: Warren's Gate. Inside the entrance is an ascending passageway 18 feet (5.5 m) wide and 85 feet (26 m) long with a flight of stairs that at some point was converted into a cistern.

The next gate no longer exists, only remnants of the arches that supported a causeway onto which this upper gate opened. Another British explorer, Charles Wilson, discovered the monumental arch adjoining the western wall. Today the arch and the gate that rested above it are called by his name: Wilson's Gate. As Josephus describes, the passageway bridged the Tyropoeon Valley, "it led to the palace by a passage over the intervening ravine" (cf. *Ant.* 15:410). The palace described by Josephus was the Hasmonean Palace. The bridge provided access for the Hasmonean priests from the western hill to the Temple Mount and also supported the aqueduct that brought water from south of Jerusalem. Wilson's Gate may be identified with what the Mishnah calls Coponius' Gate, seemingly named for the first Roman procurator (*Ant.* 18:2; *J.W.* 2:117). While mention of the gate in the tractate *Middot* may suggest it was not part of Herod's renovations, its name indicates that it was named after the Roman procurator, who assumed power after the brief rule of Archelaus, Herod's son.

King Agrippa II built a large dining room in the Hasmonean Palace, which Josephus locates "near to the Xystos" (*Ant.* 20:189). The Greek term means polished colonnade, which suggests that it designates a colonnaded plaza on the western hill. Descriptions of the Xystos near the Hasmonean

Palace locate both near where the bridge joined the eastern slopes of the western hill. In the days preceding the Jewish Revolt, Agrippa sought to dissuade the Jews from open conflict with the Romans.

> He, accordingly, summoned the people to the Xystos and placed his sister Bernice in a commanding position on the roof of the palace of the Hasmoneans, which stood above the Xystos on the side opposite to the Upper City; the Xystos was connected with the temple by a bridge. (*J.W.* 2:344)

*Barclay's Gate.* (from J. T. Barclay, *The City of the Great King; Or, Jerusalem as it was, as it is, and as it is to be*, 1858)

Of course, Agrippa's appeal was unsuccessful. Later internal dissension among the Jewish partisans gave way to open conflict. Simon son of Giora rallied his faction against those allied with John of Gischala, who had control of the temple precincts. To offset the advantage of elevation, Simon built four towers surrounding the temple.

> One at the northeast corner, the second above the Xystos, the third at the corner opposite the Lower City. The last erected above the roof of the priests' chambers, at the point where it was the custom for one of the priests to stand and to give notice, by sound of trumpet, in the afternoon of the approach, and on the following evening of the close, of every seventh day, announcing to the people the respective hours for ceasing work and for resuming their labors. (*J.W.* 4:581–582; cf. *b. Shabb.* 35b; *y. Shabb.* 17.16a)

We will consider more fully below one of the more remarkable discoveries from excavations below the southwest corner of the Temple Mount—a stone corner piece inscribed "to the place of the trumpeting." For our current interest its importance is that it confirms Josephus' location of the priests' chamber on the southwestern corner of the outer walls of the precinct. From the roof of this priests' chamber one could signal the Upper City and the Lower City. Its location also suggests that Simon's second tower lay "above" the Xystos on the western side of the Temple Mount.

On the south side of today's Western Wall plaza, currently a place of Jewish devotion, is the second lower gate: Barclay's Gate, named after the American missionary doctor, James Barclay, who discovered it. The gate was oriented like its partner (i.e., Warren's Gate) to lead to the suburbs outside of the temple courts. It opened onto the Herodian street that followed the Tyropoeon Valley and led to the lower city, the Pool of Siloam and the city gate exiting the city. Leen Ritmeyer has recently suggested that both Warren's Gate and Barclay's Gate led to L-shaped staircases that brought the entrant to the precincts of the temple. His conclusions are based largely on observations by nineteenth-century explorers who investigated what were thought to be cisterns, but in these instances were the subterranean passageways of the Herodian temple complex. Yet, the two differed in their approaches. Warren's Gate ascends directly to the east, while the ascent through Barclay's Gate began with a flight of stairs eastward 69 feet (21 m) and then turned to the south another 43 feet (13 m).

The final of the four western gates was named for its discoverer, the father of modern historical geography, Edward Robinson, Professor of Biblical Literature at Union Theological Seminary

*Robinson's Arch at the southwestern corner of the Temple Mount.* (photo Maureen Garcia)

in New York City. He visited the Holy Land in 1838 and Jerusalem in 1852. Robinson identified the spring of the arch protruding from the wall near the southwestern corner of the Haram. Until recent excavations it was assumed that this arch supported the bridge mentioned earlier by Josephus. However, excavations carried out under the direction of Benjamin Mazar found that the arch supported a monumental staircase leading from the Herodian street to the Royal Stoa through a high gate. Josephus describes its relationship to the Upper City, being separated by the Tyropoeon Valley. "The remaining (gate) led to the other part of the city (i.e., Upper), from which it was separated by many steps, going down to the ravine and from here up again to the hill" (*Ant.* 15:410). In Benjamin Mazar's excavations near the monumental staircase, he found the stairs mentioned by Josephus that ascended to the Upper City.

## Huldah Gates

According to rabbinic tradition, the primary ascent by pilgrims was through the Huldah Gates, "these served for coming in and for going out" (*m. Mid.* 1:3). Remains of these gates can still be seen along the southern wall of the Temple Mount, today popularly designated the Double Gate and Triple Gate. The Triple Gate lies approximately 100 feet (30.5 m) east of its pair. Most of the stones comprised in the Triple Gate result from later reconstruction. Its original design may also have been a double gate. An original Herodian doorjamb still stands *in situ*. The Mishnah fittingly describes these double-gated passageways for pilgrims, as well as for entrants who were either in mourning or rebuke:

> Whosoever it was that entered the Temple Mount came in on the right and went round and came out on the left, save any whom aught befell, for he went round to the left. "What aileth thee that thou goest to the left?" "Because I am a mourner." "May he that dwelleth in this House give thee comfort!" "Because I am under a ban." "May he that dwelleth in this House put it into their hearts to bring thee near again!" (*m. Mid.* 2:2)

Inside these gates one enters a double-vaulted entrance hall and tunnel with stairs ascending to the opening of the precincts surrounding the sanctuary. Today, this same architectural feature is retained in the steps leading up from the so-called "Solomon's Stables" under al-Aqsa Mosque to the plaza between the mosque and the Dome of the Rock.

Passing through the Huldah Gates the pilgrim moved from the heat and bright sunlight outside into the darkened, cool shelter of the double-vaulted entrance chambers. Herodian workmanship can still be seen on the stones. Ascending a short incline, one arrived at the opening onto an esplanade made of a dazzling array of colored stones (*J.W.* 5:192). The broad Court of the Gentiles was permissible to both Jews and God-fearing Gentiles.

## THE ROYAL STOA

Exiting the subterranean passageway the pilgrim faced north towards the temple. The Royal Stoa stood behind, and colonnaded porticoes ran along the eastern, western and northern perimeter of the outer precincts. According to Josephus, construction on the porticoes was part of Herod's improvements to the temple that began in 19 B.C. (*Ant.* 15:380; or 22 B.C. according to *J.W.* 1:401). The Johannine report that work continued on the temple for forty-six years (John 2:20) likely also includes the reconstruction and repairs that were necessitated by the damage done by the soldiers of Sabanus in an uprising in 4 B.C., "the legionaries [of Sabanus] set fire to the porticoes, which for massive

*The Triple Gate in the southern wall of the Temple Mount.* (photo Peter Wong)

grandeur and magnificence were wonderful works of art" (*J.W.* 2:59). Even Rabban Gamaliel the Elder, the teacher of Paul (Acts 22:3), is mentioned in connection with renovations during the first century A.D., "he used to supervise the builders" (*y. Shabb.* 16).

Josephus presents a flattering description of Herod's impressive construction of the Royal Stoa.

> The Royal Stoa had three aisles, extending in length from the eastern to the western ravine. It was not possible for it to extend farther. It was a structure more noteworthy than any under the sun…Now the columns (of the stoa) stood in four rows, one opposite the other all along—the fourth row was attached to a wall built of stone—and the thickness of each column was such that it would take three men with outstretched arms touching one another to envelop it; its height was twenty-seven feet, and there was a double moulding around its base.
>
> (*Ant.* 15:411–413)

The grandeur with which Herod adorned the surrounding porticoes and Royal Stoa may have been related to his own restriction of access to the Inner Court of the temple. Unlike his predecessors, Herod did not descend from priestly stock. He, therefore, was forbidden to even approach his own construction. Josephus mentions this limitation in his description of Herod's building. "Into none of these courts did King Herod enter, since he was not a priest and was therefore prevented from so doing. But with the contruction of the porticoes and the outer courts he did busy himself, and these he finished building in eight years" (*Ant.* 15:420).

Herod adopted the eastern architectural style of a *temenos*, a walled, open-air court with porticoes on three sides and a basilica on the remaining side. A similar design is found in Cyrene and the centers of the Roman East in Antioch and Palmyra. Typically, the basilica was comprised of four rows of columns with a central nave and two aisles. The structure was higher in the middle than the aisles, and this is indeed the depiction of the Royal Stoa of Herod.

> The number of all the columns was a hundred and sixty-two, and their capitals were ornamented in the Corinthian style of carving, which caused amazement by the magnificence of its whole effect. Since there were four rows, they made three aisles among them, under the porticoes. Of these the two side ones corresponded and were made in the same way, each being thirty feet in width, a stade in length, and over fifty feet in height. But the middle aisle was one and a half times as wide and twice as high, and thus it greatly towered over those on either side. (*Ant.* 15:414–415)

Excavations of the debris left by the Roman destruction of the Temple Mount have unearthed column drums and fragments of Corinthian capitals. These correspond to Josephus' description; however, he presents two more elements of architectural detail that challenge our modern imaginations. First, the total number of columns in the structure of four rows leaves two remaining (i.e., forty, four-column rows). Did these form a distyle porch at the western entrance to the basilica?

Further, the increased height of the columns for the

*Ceramic roof tile made by the Roman Legio X Fretensis and first introduced to Jerusalem after the destruction of the city in A.D. 70.* (on display at The Israel Museum; photo Todd Bolen)

*Remains of Corinthian capitals, in the courtyard of the Islamic Museum on the Temple Mount.* (photo Zachary Wong)

nave indicates that its roof was higher than the adjoining roofs for the two aisles. This allowed light to penetrate from above into the aisles. Most architectural reconstructions of the Royal Stoa portray it with Mediterranean styled red roof tiles, but we have no evidence for tiles used in Judea until after the Roman conquest of Jerusalem. Later, the Roman Legio X Fretensis established a tile workshop on the outskirts of the city near the site of today's International Convention Center in the modern western part of Jerusalem. Many roof tiles have been discovered with the distinctive LEG•X•Fr, signifying the Tenth Legion. As for the Royal Stoa, all three sections of roof were likely flat, not gabled as is often depicted.

> The ceilings (of the porticoes) were ornamented with deeply cut wood-carvings representing all sorts of different figures. The ceiling of the middle aisle was raised to a greater height, and the front wall was cut at either end into architraves with columns built into it, and all of it was polished, so that these structures seemed incredible to those who had not seen them and were beheld with amazement by those who set eyes on them. (*Ant.* 15:416)

Among the destruction debris archaeologists discovered in 1968 was a broken Herodian ashlar, eight feet (2.4 m) in length, which once adorned the pinnacle of the southwest corner of the temple precincts above the Royal Stoa. The violent dismantling of the monumental walls surrounding the Herodian Temple illustrates the fury of Titus' siege of Jerusalem. According to the Jewish historian Josephus Flavius, Eleazar son of Simon and his men occupied the inner courts of the temple (*J.W.* 5:5–6), while the party led by John of Gischala defended the outer courts and the lower city (*J.W.* 4:567–568; 5:9). Rome thus viewed the temple not as a sanctuary of religious piety, but a stronghold of rebellion that lay at the center of the Jewish insurrection.

As mentioned previously, archaeologists discovered a peculiar niche cut into the ornate ashlar as a place for someone to stand. Together with a fragmentary inscription cut into the stone, excavators were able to identify the stone's original placement. The Hebrew inscription begins, "To the place of the trumpeting...." Josephus in his description of the four towers built by the Zealots atop the walls surrounding the temple reports,

…the last was erected above the roof of the priests' chambers, at the point where it was the custom for one of the priests to stand and give notice, by sound of trumpet, in the afternoon of the approach and on the following evening of the close, of every seventh day, announcing to the people the respective hours for ceasing work and for resuming their labors. (*J.W.* 4:582)

The historian's description of the actions of the priests to signal for the citizens of Jerusalem the onset and close of the Sabbath parallels a similar description in *Mishnah Sukkah* 5:5: "On the eve of the Sabbath [the priests] used to blow six more blasts, three to cause the people to cease from work and three to distinguish between the sacred and the profane."

Scholars have speculated how the broken line of the inscription would have continued. Two letters are visible before the break, *lamed* and *heh*. What follows is a partial letter. Typically this last letter has been identified as a *kaf*, with suggestions that the next word should be read *l'ha-kohen* (for the priest), *l'hekhal* (to the temple), or *l'hakhriz* (to herald [the Sabbath]). Others follow Aaron Demsky who has proposed that the broken letter is a *bet*, and his reconstructed reading that continues, *l'habdil* (*to distinguish between*, i.e., the sacred and the profane), which reflects the Mishnaic wording cited above. The inscription would thus mark the place where the priest stood to blow the trumpet and signal for the people of Jerusalem the beginning and end of the sacred day. While scholars differ in their reconstruction of the inscription, all agree concerning the stone's identification with "the place of the trumpeting," and the centrality of the temple and its priests in regulating the rhythm of life in first-century Jerusalem.

*(above) Stone of the Trumpeting Place, discovered at the southwestern corner of the Temple Mount and (below) reconstruction of the inscription proposed by A. Demsky, ending in* l'habdil.

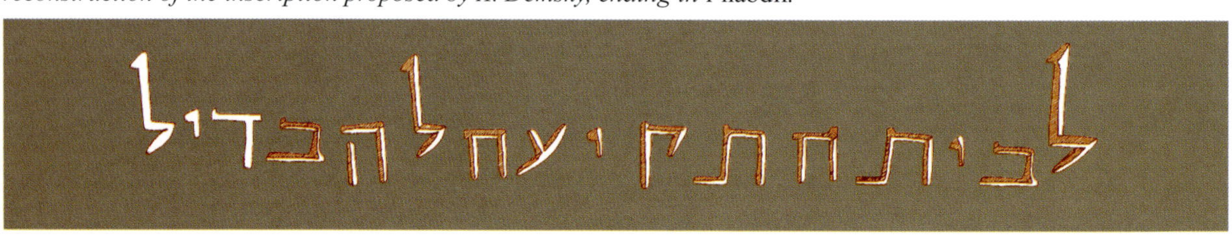

CHAPTER 10

# Administration of the Temple: Priests and Levites

For much of the Hellenistic period Judea was ruled as a hierocracy. The political control of the priests was such that the Greek historian Hecataeus of Abdera assumed the Jewish nation had no need for a king: "For this reason, the Jews never have a king, and authority over the people is regularly vested in whichever priest is regarded as superior to his colleagues in wisdom and virtue" (Diod. Sic. 40.3.5). The priests in this early period belonged to the family of Zadok and the watch of Jedaiah. In spite of Hecataeus' suggestion that the high priest was selected solely according to his merit, normally the position passed from father to son. If no sons were available, the high priesthood fell to another member of the family. Traditionally, the high priest served until his death, but this practice changed under Antiochus IV Epiphanes. He introduced the Hellenistic practice of appointing a priest temporarily and usually influenced by the candidate's contribution to the royal treasury. This and other foreign practices contributed to the agitation that erupted in the Hasmonean Revolt (167–164 B.C.).

The dominance of the priestly class reached its height with the Hasmoneans, a family of priests from the watch of Jehoiarib. Under their leadership the nation was eventually able to achieve political independence from Seleucid domination under Simon in 141 B.C. While his brother Jonathan had been appointed high priest by the Syrian usurper, Alexander Balas, the people themselves acclaimed Simon high priest, when it was mistakenly assumed that Jonathan was already dead.

> The Jews and their priests have resolved that Simon should be their leader and high priest forever, until a trustworthy prophet should arise, and that he should be governor over them and that he should take charge of the sanctuary and appoint officials over its tasks and over the country and the weapons and the strongholds, and that he should take charge of the sanctuary, and that he should be obeyed by all, and that all contracts in the country should be written in his name.… All the people agreed to grant Simon the right to act in accordance with these decisions. So Simon accepted and agreed to be high priest, to be commander and ethnarch of the Jews and priests, and to be protector of them all. (1 Macc 14:41–47)

Later, one of Simon's grandsons (Judah Aristobulus or Alexander Jannaeus) was the first priest to assume the title king. However, it is also during this period that we begin to hear criticism of the abuses of power by the high priests in Jerusalem's Temple. The Hasmoneans ignored the Old Testament restriction of powers between the king, priests and prophets.

Ultimately, it was Herod who was responsible for bringing an end to the political power of the

Hasmoneans. He deposed the last of the Hasmonean rulers, Antigonus son of Aristobulus II, and was also rumored to be responsible for the death of his nephew, Alexander, the last of the Hasmoneans to serve as high priest. Under King Herod the dynastic passing of the high priesthood ceased. They were once again appointed at the discretion of the king. So also ended the previous practice reinstated during the Hasmonean period that the high priest served for life.

When Herod's son Archelaus was deposed by the Romans, appointment of the high priest fell to the Roman governors. This remained the custom until the final years of the Second Temple. During the renewal of the Herodian dynasty under Agrippa I, Herod of Chalcis and Agrippa II, responsibility for the appointment of the high priest once again rested with the Jewish rulers. Wealthy priestly families dominated the high priesthood. One of these was the longest dynastic priestly family in the Roman period, the house of Hanin (Annas). Its family members are mentioned in the New Testament, Josephus and rabbinic literature. In the Talmud they appear with other prominent priestly families as the authors of abuse and closely aligned with the Romans (cf. *b. Pesah.* 57a; *t. Menah.* 13:21).

While the high priesthood during the final decades of the Second Temple was controlled by the upper classes, this does not characterize all priests. Most priests lived outside of Jerusalem, in the towns and villages of Judea, Galilee, the Transjordan and elsewhere in the Diaspora. Unlike the high priests of this period, they did not belong to the Sadducees, but often were Pharisees and Essenes. Some were even numbered among the Zealots. During the Jewish revolt against Rome, the Zealots deposed the previous aristocratic high priests and appointed Phineas b. Samuel, a

*The tomb of the high priest Annas, located in the Hinnom Valley, is situated near the "Refuge of the Apostles," photographed here in 1853.* (photo A. Salzmann)

stonemason by profession and relative by marriage to the family of Hillel the Great.

The Levites played a diminishing role in the temple service in the Greco-Roman period. After the return from Exile, they are mentioned together with the priests in the dedication of the temple (Ezra 6:16–18; Neh 12:44). Yet, they are absent from the report of the Hasmonean rededication of the temple in the Hellenistic period (1 Macc 4:36–57). Ben Sira's brief mention of the divine service also makes no mention of the Levites (Sir 50:12–13). It seems that from the Hellenistic period Levites were relegated to an inferior status and served as mere singers, musicians and gatekeepers (*m. Mid.* 1:1–2; *m. Tamid* 7:3). In this final task they were assigned to open and close the gates and assure that those entering the temple courts were ritually clean. Levites receive scant mention in the New Testament. Jesus describes a Levite departing Jerusalem on the road to Jericho (Luke 10:32), a depiction that perhaps reflects the twenty-four rotating courses of Levites. Similar to many priests, these Levites often lived outside of Jerusalem and journeyed to the temple to fulfill their ministration. Barnabas, the companion of Paul, is described as a Levite and native of Cyprus (Acts 4:36), an example of the presence of Levites in the Jewish diaspora. Almost all of Josephus' references to Levites concern their service in the earlier biblical period. The only exceptions are a passing reference to Levites in the days of Onias (*Ant.* 13:73) and a dispute during the reign of King Agrippa II.

> Those of the Levites—this is one of our tribes—who were singers of hymns urged the king to convene the Sanhedrin and get them permission to wear linen robes on equal terms with the priest, maintaining that it was fitting that he should introduce, to mark his reign, some innovation by which he would be remembered. Nor did they fail to obtain their request; for the king, with the consent of those who attended the Sanhedrin, allowed the singers of hymns to discard their former robes and to wear linen ones such as they wished. (*Ant.* 20:216–217)

The importance given to levitical tasks in the Dead Sea Scrolls contributed to the increased prominence and role of Levites in the present and future hopes of the Qumran Congregation.

## THE DIVINE SERVICE

The temple service was a focal point for Jewish faith in late antiquity. According to Simeon the Righteous, "Upon three things the world stands: the Law, temple service and deeds of loving-kindness" (*m. Avot* 1:2). Responsibility for the daily sacrificial rites belonged to the priests, who were divided into twenty-four rotating courses that lasted a week at a time. The Levites and the nation were also divided into twenty-four courses; however, while the priests and Levites were required to fulfill their service in the temple, the people were not expected to travel to Jerusalem during their course. Instead, they gathered in local synagogues for prayer and reading from the Scriptures (*m. Ta'an.* 4:1–4), while a representative delegation attended the offering of the sacrifices in Jerusalem.

Daily sacrifices consisted of both public and private offerings. The former was paid for by dues, especially the annual half-shekel temple tax (cf. *m. Sheqal.* 1:1; Exod 30:13; cf. *Ant.* 3:194; 18:312; Matt 17:24–27). Sacrifices took place in the Inner Court and consisted of burnt offerings, sin offerings and peace offerings. The most important part of the daily temple service was the whole burnt-offering (the *Tamid*). Its actual practice changed over time, but by the time of the Second Temple the *Tamid* was offered twice daily (1 Chr 16:40; 2 Chr 8:12; 31:3). Other free-will and obligatory offerings were carried out between the two whole burnt-offerings. Continuation of the burnt-offerings was considered so important that even when Jerusalem was under Roman siege and the city's population starving, the

## THE TWENTY-FOUR PRIESTLY DIVISIONS

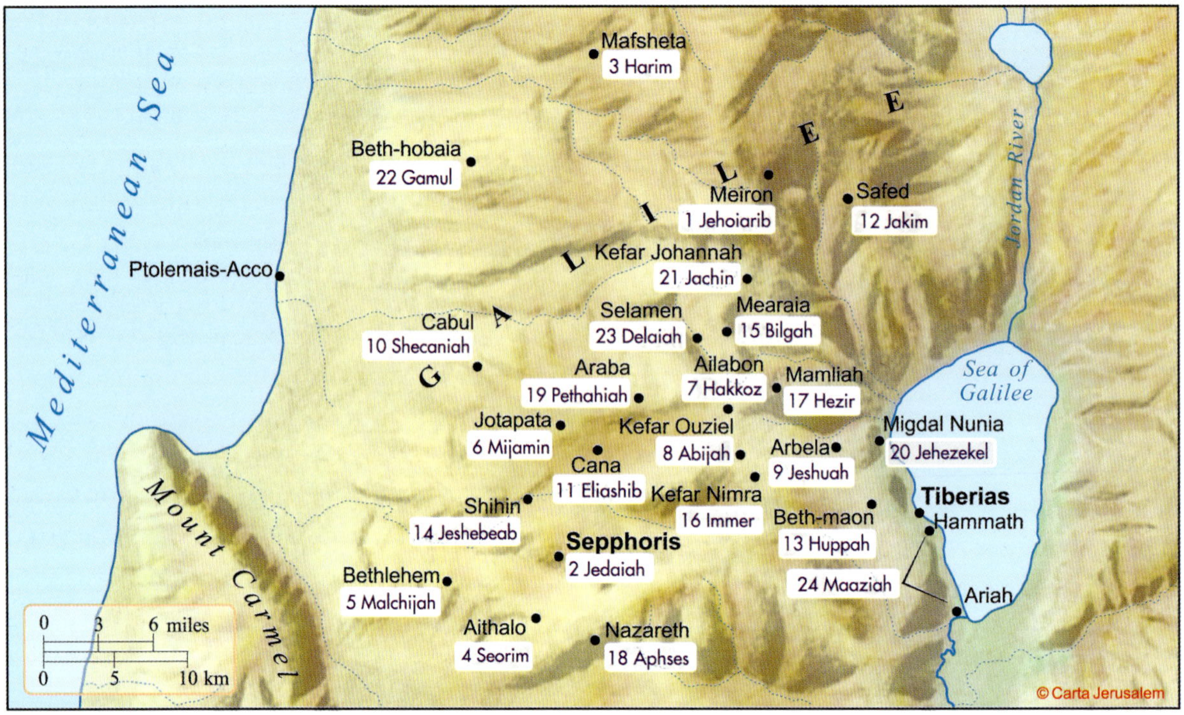


whole burnt-offering was maintained (*Ant.* 3:318–321). It was considered a national tragedy when the daily offering was disrupted (*J.W.* 6:94–95; *m. Ta'an.* 4:6; *b. Sotah* 49b; cf. Dan 8:11–13; 11:31; 12:11).

The whole burnt-offering was celebrated in the morning and evening, accompanied by stringed instruments, trumpets by two priests, and the singing of fixed daily psalms by the Levites.

> This was the singing that the Levites used to sing in the Temple. On the first day they sang, "The earth is the Lord's, and everything in it, the world, and all who live in it" (Ps 24); on the second day they sang, "Great is the Lord, and most worthy of praise, in the city of our God, his holy mountain" (Ps 48); on the third day they sang, "God presides in the great assembly; he gives judgment among the 'gods'" (Ps 82); on the fourth day they sang, "O Lord, the God who avenges, O God who avenges, shine forth" (Ps 94); on the fifth day they sang, "Sing for joy to God our strength; shout aloud to the God of Jacob" (Ps 81); on the sixth day they sang, "The Lord reigns, he is robed in majesty" (Ps 93). On the Sabbath they sang, "A psalm. A song. For the Sabbath day" (Ps 92); a Psalm, a song for the time that is to come, for the day that shall be all Sabbath and rest in the life everlasting.
>
> (*m. Tamid* 7:4)

In accordance with the prescriptions from Numbers 15:1–16, a grain offering and a drink offering accompanied the burnt-offering.

Most priests did not live in Jerusalem but traveled to the holy city to complete their service in the temple. During the week of their service, they slept in the temple precincts (*m. Yoma* 1:4). Regular priests served on ordinary days, and the high priest officiated the sacrifices on Sabbaths and feast days. The officiating priest was clothed in special vestments in accordance with the biblical instruction: trousers, tunic, sash and turban (Exod 28:40–43; 39:27–29; *Ant.* 3:151–158; cf. Philo *Vita Moses* 2:45; Ezek 44:17–19).

Prior to the morning whole burnt-offering and following its pair in the evening, an allotted priest entered the temple for the offering of incense. "The morning incense was offered between [the sprinkling of] the blood and [the offering of] the parts; the evening incense between [the offering

*Half-shekel coin which was found on the Temple Mount with evidence of having been in a fire. So, we may have in hand an offering that was in the Temple itself when it was burnt. For New Testament concerns, the half-shekel tax is not mentioned in the Hebrew Scriptures. It is a post-biblical development. Further it was not universally accepted. Jesus' willingness to pay the tax* (*Matt 17:24–27*) *is yet another indication that he was closer to the approach of the Pharisees, who accepted the practice, than the Essenes who rejected it.* (Courtesy of Zachi Dvira)

of] the parts and the drink-offerings" (*m. Yoma* 3:5; cf. Exod 30:7, 8; Philo *Spec. Let.* 1:171, 276). The priest who was privileged to perform the incense offering was chosen by lot from among those who had come to fulfill their priestly course, and upon whom the lot had never previously fallen. "He said to them: You that are new to the incense preparation, come and cast lots" (*m. Tamid* 5:2).

The description of the selection of the priest in the Mishnaic tractate *Tamid* is also reflected in Luke's account. "Once when Zechariah's division was on duty and he was serving as priest before God, he was chosen by lot, according to the custom of the priesthood, to go into the temple of the Lord and burn incense" (Luke 1:8–9). Reports of heavenly revelations to Zacharias (Luke 1:9–20) and John Hyrcanus (*Ant.* 13:282) at the time of their ministration of the incense offering are fitting, because this rite was considered the most solemn part of the daily sacrificial service.

Ordinary daily sacrifices were supplemented on Sabbaths, new moons and the feast days of Passover, Pentecost and Tabernacles. Restrictions for service inherent in the priestly courses were set aside during the festivals, so that any eligible priest was permitted to participate in the festal offerings. The public nature of these offerings also shifted the normally exclusive role for priests to the people, as the laity served a more active role. According to sources, even the veil concealing the inner sanctuary of the temple was pulled back and the sacred vessels brought out to the Inner Court for the people to see (*m. Hag.* 3:8; *P.Oxy.* 5:840).

The central feature of the feast of Passover was the slaughter of the paschal lamb by groups of pilgrims, rather than by the priests (*m. Pesah.* 5:6; *y. Pesah.* 6:33a; Philo *Spec.* 2:145; *QE* 1:10). There are indications that a quorum of ten men was required to offer the paschal sacrifice (*m. Pesah.* 8:7; *Tg. Ps.-J.* on Exod 12:4; *J.W.* 6:423–433; *t. Pesah.* 4:3), but literary witnesses also describe groups that included women, children and even slaves (*m. Pesah.* 8:7; 9:8).

The ancient agricultural origins of the biblical feasts are reflected in their offerings. Passover celebrated the barley harvest, and the beginning of "the counting of the *'omer*" with the waving the sheaves (i.e., the *'omer*) of barley. Seven weeks later, the Feast of Weeks (Exod 34:22; Num 28:26; or *Pentecost* as it is called in Hellenistic Jewish sources: Tob 2:1; 2 Macc 12:31–32; *Ant.* 3:252; *J.W.* 1:253) commemorated the wheat harvest. "And you shall count from the morrow after the sabbath, from the day that you brought the sheaf (*'omer*) of the wave offering; seven full weeks shall they be, counting fifty days to the morrow after the seventh sabbath; then you shall present a cereal offering of new grain to the Lord" (Lev 23:15–16). On the day of Pentecost two wheat-loaves were presented as a food offering to mark the holiday (Lev 23:15–22).

## SUPPLIES TO THE TEMPLE AND THE BRINGING OF THE *'OMER*

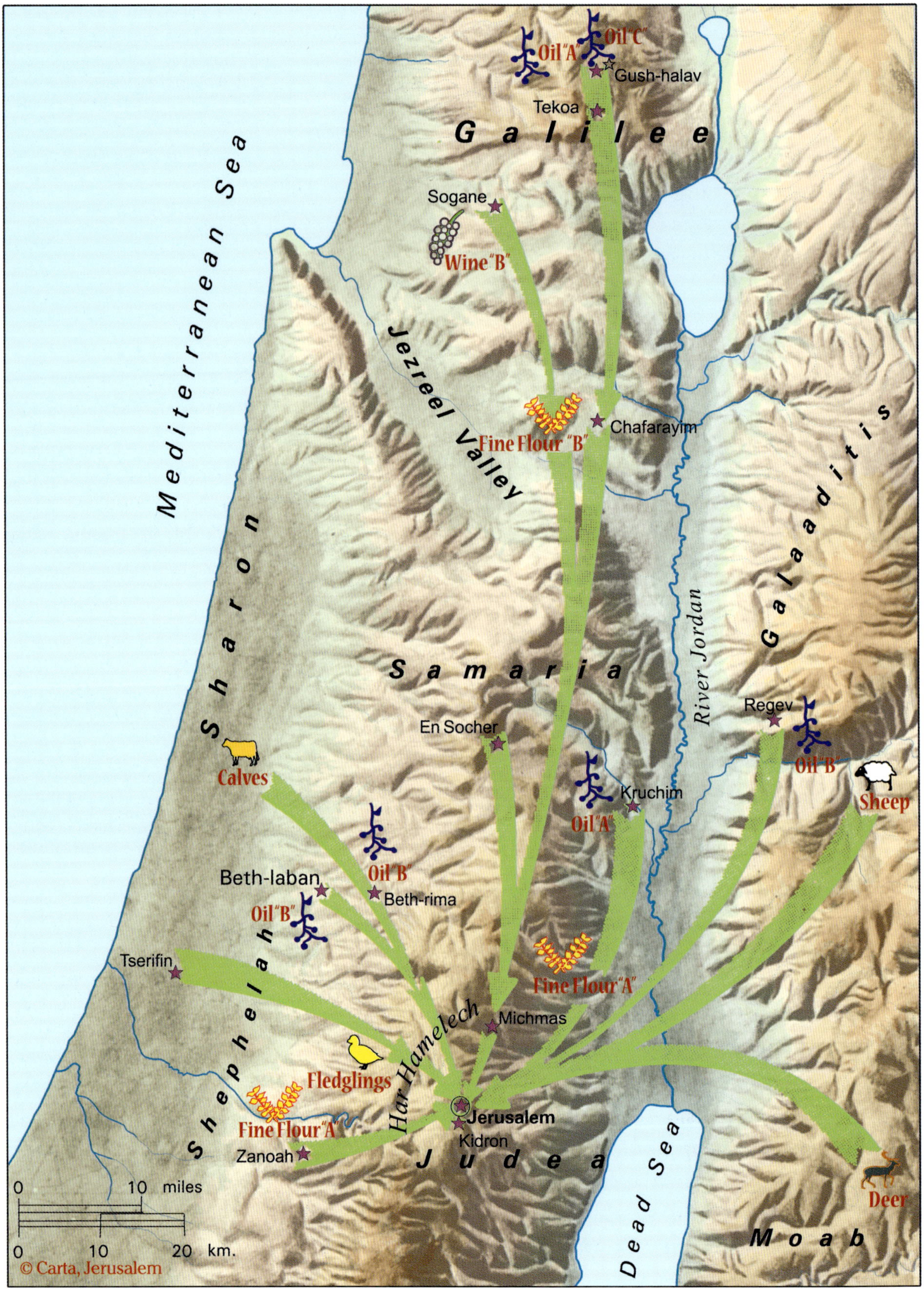

The biblical description that Moses ascended to Sinai "in the third month" (Exod 19:1–6), the same month in which the Feast of Weeks occurs, likely contributed to the early identification of Pentecost with the giving of the Torah at Sinai. Scholars debate how early this identification began, and whether it could have served as the religious backdrop for Luke's report about the events on Pentecost in Acts 2. The question of Luke's literary allusions aside, the author of the Book of Jubilees (2nd century B.C.) certainly had Pentecost in mind in his opening, "In the first year of the Exodus of the children of Israel from Egypt, in *the third month on the sixteenth day* of that month, the Lord spoke to Moses, saying, 'Come up to me on the mountain, and I shall give you two stone tablets of the Law and the commandment, which I have written, so that you may teach them'" (Jub 1:1).

The third of the three yearly pilgrimage feasts, the Feast of Tabernacles, marked the autumn harvest (Exod 23:16; 34:22; Lev 23:34–36, 39–43; Num 29:12–38; Deut 16:13–15) and at the same time remembered the wilderness wanderings (Lev 23:42–43). In the Hebrew Scriptures the holiday is sometimes simply called "the Feast" (1 Kgs 8:2, 65; 12:32; Ezek 42:25; Neh 8:14; 2 Chr 5:3), and this designation continued in post-biblical writings (e.g., John 7:37). The holiday was characterized by its festivity with the singing of the *Hallel* on all eight days of the celebration (*m. Arak.* 2:3; *y. Sukkah* 5:55a). As with Passover and Pentecost, the people participated in the rites of Tabernacles, including their procession with palm branches around the altar, an area usually restricted to all but the priests (*m. Sukkah* 4:5).

A peculiar rite associated with Tabernacles was the water libations, which began from the evening of the first day of the Feast and was repeated each night for eight days. Large gatherings celebrated at night in the temple courts. These included priests, Levites and pilgrims who proceeded together at dawn to the pool of Siloam to draw water for the libations on the altar in the Inner Court of the temple. In the sabbatical year, the community was also convened on the last day of the Feast for the reading of the Torah (*m. Sotah* 7:8; *t. Sotah* 7:13–17; *Ant.* 4:209–211). This was in fulfillment of the instruction in Deuteronomy 31:10–13: "And Moses commanded them, 'At the end of every seven years, at the set time of the year of release, at the feast of booths, when all Israel comes to appear before the Lord your God at the place which he will choose, you shall read this law before all Israel in their hearing....'"

The Day of Atonement was considered the most solemn of the temple rites. The special offering could only be made by the high priest, who began seven days prior to prepare for ritual duties. He was responsible for the offering of the whole burnt-offering, the additional offerings and entrance into the holy of holies for the burning of the incense. Additional rites included the burning of the heifer and the release of the scapegoat into the Judean wilderness. These could be performed by other priests and the laity. The biblical direction to "deny [lit., *afflict*] yourselves" (Lev 23:27, 32; cf. Num 29:7) was later understood to mean fasting, and the denial of other physical pleasures (*m. Yoma* 8:1; CD 6:19). Fasting became so identified with the day that the Dead Sea Scrolls (1QpHab 11:8), Josephus (*Ant.* 18:94) and the New Testament (Acts 27:9) all simply refer to the day as "the Fast day." In the faith of the Qumran Congregation, the day was associated not only with atonement, but hoped-for redemption (4Q508 f2:2). This undoubtedly is related to their expectation of the advent of a priestly redeemer bringing redemption in the Jubilee year (11Q13 2:4–13). It certainly was not missed by these sectarians that according to Leviticus 25:9–10 the Jubilee began on the Day of Atonement:

> [He (i.e., Melchizedek) shall pro]claim this decree in the fir[s]t [wee]k of the Jubilee period that foll[ows nine j]ubilee periods. Then the "D[ay of Atone]ment" shall follow af[ter] the [te]nth [ju]bilee period, when he shall atone for all the Sons of [Light] and the peopl[e who are pre]destined to Mel[chi]zedek [...]. (11Q13 2:6–8)

Finally, brief mention should be made regarding the daily offerings in the Jerusalem temple in honor of the Roman emperor. As was widely recognized in the ancient world, worship of foreign deities was forbidden for Jews. At least from the time of Julius Caesar and Augustus Jews living in the diaspora were exempted from participation in the imperial cult (cf. *Ant.* 16:162–165). Those same freedoms were extended to Jews living in Judea, and great care was taken not to disturb Jewish sensibilities regarding its strict monotheism. A client king of Rome, Herod was careful in his introduction of the imperial cult within the borders of his kingdom. Josephus reports that Herod built temples in honor of Augustus, but these were only constructed in two cities that were newly founded (Caesarea and Sebaste) and in Paneas, whose majority population were non-Jews. In so doing, Herod avoided introducing the new practice in long-settled, predominantly Jewish settings. Israel's Sages were certainly aware of Herod's temples to Augustus. Yet, it could be maintained with confidence, "Never in our generation, nor in these present days, has there been any tribe or family or people or town of ours that worships gods made with hands, as was done in days gone by" (Jdt 8:18; cf. *b. Yoma* 69b; *b. Sanh.* 64a; *b. Arak.* 32b; *Shir Rab.* 1:17; 7:8).

The beginnings of the practice of offerings in Jerusalem's temple in honor of the Roman emperor are unknown. While it may have begun under Herod, it seems more likely that it resulted from the dissolution of Herod's kingdom with the deposition of his son, Archelaus, and Judea becoming a Roman province. The first explicit mention is during the reign of Gaius (*Ant.* 18:124). There was precedence for honoring temporal rulers (Ezra 6:10; Jer 29:7; 1 Macc 7:33; Bar 1:10–12). Rather than offerings to the emperor that were given regularly in other provinces, Josephus and Philo report of the daily sacrifices in Jerusalem's temple of two lambs and a bull for the emperor's well being (*Legat.* 157, 232, 317; *Ag. Ap.* 2:77; *J.W.* 2:197, 409). Later, Josephus remarked that the cessation of this sacrifice was "the foundation stone of the war with Rome" (*J.W.* 2:409–410; cf. *b. Git.* 56a; *Midr. Lam R.* 4.2.3; *t. Shabb.* 16.17.8).

## THE BALUSTRADE

While still in the outer Court of the Gentiles, pilgrims circled the Inner Court of the temple and prostrated thirteen times before entering. The colonnaded porticoes of the outer court were 49 feet (15 m) high and their cedar roofs were supported by two rows of white limestone columns, each rising 39 feet (12 m) in height (*J.W.* 5:190). The width of the porticoes was the same as their height. Here pilgrims gathered out of the sun, studied and talked of current events. According to rabbinic sources, on the mount were also synagogues and "houses of study" in which the Scriptures were discussed (beth midrash: *t. Sanh.* 7:1; *t. Hag.* 2:9; synagogue: *m. Yoma* 7:1; *m. Sotah* 7:8; see Luke 2:46–47).

The Court of the Gentiles was separated from the central Court of Israel by a balustrade (Hebrew: *soreg*). It was comprised of short, 5-foot (1.5-m) pillars that were linked by stone slabs. There were thirteen openings for passage between the two courts (*m. Mid.* 2:3) with an inscription in Greek and Latin warning that unwitting Gentiles who passed beyond the barricade were responsible for their own punishment (see *m. Kelim* 1:8; *Ant.* 15:417; *J.W.* 5:194). Remnants of two of these warning inscriptions have been found. A fragmentary one is on exhibit at the Israel Museum in Jerusalem and a complete example is on display at the National Archaeological Museum in Istanbul, Turkey.

*Greek inscription banning Gentiles from entering the sanctified area of the Temple Mount.* (photo R. Steven Notley)

The inscription reads: "No foreigner may enter within the barricade that surrounds the sanctuary and enclosure. Anyone who is caught doing so will have himself to blame for his ensuing death" (cf. *J.W.* 6:124–126).

The Apostle Paul's arrest in the temple was precipitated on the accusation of bringing a non-Jew beyond the balustrade into the Court of Israel.

> When the seven days [completing the Nazirite vow] were nearly over, some Jews from the province of Asia saw Paul at the temple. They stirred up the whole crowd and seized him, shouting, "Men of Israel, help us! This is the man who teaches all men everywhere against our people and our law and this place. And besides, he has brought Greeks into the temple area and defiled this holy place." They had previously seen Trophimus the Ephesian in the city with Paul and assumed that Paul had brought him into the temple area. (Acts 21:27–29)

This balustrade is also the metaphor the Apostle Paul had in mind when he spoke spiritually of the separation between Jews and Gentiles that was brought to an end in Christ's death: "For he himself is our peace, who has made the two one and has destroyed the barrier, *the dividing wall* of hostility" (Eph 2:14).

Moving beyond the balustrade, the Jewish supplicant ascended fourteen (*m. Mid.* 2:3) [or twelve: *J.W.* 6:195] steps to a landing that was 16.4 feet (5 m) wide. This narrow platform known as the *Hel* surrounded the wall of the temple enclosure. Towers surmounted the wall on its four corners. This internal precinct was divided into two large courts: the Court of the Women on the east (*J.W.* 5:199, 206; 6:415; *m. Sukkah* 5:2,4; *m. Mid.* 2:5, 6; *m. Kelim* 1:8) and the Inner Court on the west. These two courts were surrounded by a large wall with seven entrances, six of which provided limited access into the Inner Court for priests.

However, pilgrims entered the Inner Court from the east through a gate leading from the Court of the Women. Entrance from the east into the Court of the Women was through a large gate that stood 82 feet (25 m) high. Its portals were covered with gold and silver plates, suggesting to some that this was the "gate called beautiful" described in Acts 3:2. The Court of the Women was square, measuring 221.5 feet (67.5 m) on its sides and possessing four chambers. Each chamber was comprised of a small portico surrounding an open court. On the northwest was the Chamber of the Lepers with a *miqveh* for ritual purification (*m. Mid.* 2:5; *t. Neg.* 8:9; cf. Luke 5:14); on the northeast the Chamber of Wood where wood was stored for the altar fire; on the southwest the Chamber of the House of Oils where the temple oil was kept; and fourthly on the southeast, the Chamber of the Nazirites, where the votives waited the final hours of their vows when they would shave their heads, throw their hair into a fire and present an offering (cf. Acts 21:24).

All of the communal functions relating to the divine service took place in the Court of the Women. Here the Scriptures were read on the Day of Atonement (*b. Yoma* 69b), the pouring out of the water at the conclusion of the Feast of Tabernacles (*m. Sukkah* 5:1–4), and once every seven years the king would read the Law to the people (*b. Sotah* 41b). The name Court of the Women is assumed by some scholars to indicate that it was for women only, or that women were limited to this area and could proceed no further. Instead, the nomenclature for the precinct's name likely stems from a balcony that surrounded the four sides of the court, where women assembled to witness the celebration on the feast days. Although minimally attested, there is evidence to suggest that women were permitted to continue to the Court of Israel to offer sacrifices (cf. *t. Arak.* 2:1).

Continuing westward from the Court of the Women, it was necessary to ascend fifteen steps, "rounded like the half of a round threshing-floor" (*m. Mid.* 2:5; *m. Sukkah* 5:4), because the Inner Court was 25 feet (7.5 m) higher than the Court of the Women. On these steps the Levites played instruments during the libations of water (*t. Sukkah* 4:1; *m. Mid.* 2:5). Here also they sang the Psalms of Ascents (Pss. 120–134). Lepers were placed here and declared clean; women suspected of adultery were brought here and charged (*t. Neg.* 8:9; *m. Tamid* 5:6; *m. Sotah* 1:5; cf. John 7:53–8:11). Supplicants passed through the legendary triple-door Nicanor Gate. On the lintel above the central door was a conch. The gate derived its name from its Alexandrian artisan, and the beauty of its bronze doors was such that it was decided not to regild it with gold and silver like the others, but to leave its workmanship for the passing multitudes to see and marvel (*m. Mid.* 2:3; *J.W.* 5:201–204). Its transport from Egypt to Jerusalem was the stuff of legends.

> They say: When Nicanor was bringing them from Alexandria, in Egypt, a gale rose in the sea and threatened to drown them. They took one of them and tossed it into the sea, and they wanted to throw in the other but Nicanor would not let them. He said to them, "If you throw in the second one, throw me in with it." He was distressed all the way to the wharf at Jaffa. Once they reached the wharf at Jaffa, the other door popped up from underneath the boat. (*t. Yoma* 2:4; *y. Yoma* 41a)

The historical kernel in the story, namely the identification that Nicanor of Alexandria was responsible for the gates of the Jerusalem temple, was bolstered by a discovery at the end of the nineteenth century (cf. *m. Mid.* 1:4; 2:3, 6; *m. Sheqal.* 6:3; *m. Yoma* 3:10; *m. Sotah* 1:5; *m. Neg.* 14:8; cf. Buechler 1898–1899: 46–63). A first-century ossuary found in a family tomb on Mount Scopus in Jerusalem was inscribed, "the remains of the children of Nicanor of Alexandria who made the doors."

Jews who were not priests were allowed limited access to the Inner Court. A five-meter-wide corridor along the eastern edge of the Inner Court was designated the Court of Israel. Here suppliants were permitted to offer sacrifices and approach the altars in connection with ritual practices. Facing the temple, on the left or southern half of the Inner Court stood the altar for burnt offerings. It was a horned altar, and the priest ascended it by way of a ramp from its southern side. Opposite the altar on the right-hand side was the slaughterhouse in the northern portion of the Inner Court.

The dimensions of the Inner Court were 307 feet (93.5 m) long by 220 feet (67.5 m) wide. According to the tractate *Middot* 1:4–5 six gates, three from the north and three from the south, allowed priestly access without going through the Court of the Women. From east to west on the south were the Water Gate, the Gate of the Firstlings, the Gate of the Kindling; and on the north (east to west), the Gate of the Flame and the Offering Gate. The name of the last gate on the northwest corner of the Inner Court is not recorded but provided access to the Chamber of the Hearth. There were also chambers for the priests within the porticoes that surrounded the Inner Court. These were for storage and activities related to the functions of the temple. On the southeast corner was located the *Lishkat ha-Gazit* or Chamber of Hewn Stone, one of the three reported gathering places for the Sanhedrin. It stood in both the Court of Israel and the Court of the Priests (*J.W.* 5:200; *m. Mid.* 1).

Behind the Court of Israel and standing midway in the Inner Court rose the temple itself. "The Sanctuary was narrow behind and wide in front, and it was like to a lion, as it is written, Oh Ariel, Ariel, the city where David encamped!" (*m. Mid.* 4:7; cf. Isa 29:1). The Mishnah drew from the meaning of the Hebrew term Ariel, "lion of God," to describe the shape of the Sanctuary wide in front and narrow in back, like a crouching lion. The eastern front façade of the temple was 164 feet (50 m)

*Sarcophagus of Nicanor, found on Mount Scopus.* (photo Peter Wong)

*Bar Kokhba coin with a depiction of the Temple facade (left).* (photo Zachary Wong)

wide and 164 feet (50 m) high, while its western face where the Holy of Holies was located was only 115 feet (35 m) wide.

Four half-columns decorated the entrance to the temple. This architectural feature can be seen in the coins of the Bar Kokhba revolt (*m. Mid.* 3:7; *J.W.* 5:208). The priest approached the Sanctuary, ascending twelve steps onto a porch 66 feet (20 m) wide between the two central columns. Upon these steps the priests would stand when they blessed the people (*m. Mid.* 3; *m. Tamid* 1:4). The lintel over the entrance was constructed of alternating wood and stone. The cornice was topped by battlements and gilded spikes to prevent birds from sitting on the temple parapet (*J.W.* 5:244; *m. Mid.* 4:6). According to the Talmudic tractate *Sukkah* the walls of the Temple were constructed of blue, red and white marble, veined "like the waves of the Sea" (*b. Sukkah* 51b).

The entrance was not closed by a door but a large veil of red, blue and purple colors and ornamented with a zodiac (*J.W.* 5:212; *b. Yoma* 54a). Moving past the curtain one approached the central doors of the hall that were covered with gold plating and conches. Over the doors was an ornate large vine of gold, an expression of the generosity of the people (*Ant.* 14:34–36; *J.W.* 5:211; *m. Mid.* 3:8; cf. Luke 21:5). These doors were opened during the day revealing walls covered by gold plates with palm designs. In the room stood the table for the bread of the divine presence, the golden Menorah, and the golden altar for incense. At the western end of the hall, separated by a veil, was the area of the Holy of Holies, a cubed space of 29.5 feet (9 m), which was accessible only by the high priest once a year on the Day of Atonement. Along the outer sides of the sanctuary were three tiers of cells, accessed by a ramp. There existed an upper story in the temple, but it was merely empty space and only served to raise the height of the sanctuary to 164 feet (50 m).

(photo Shmuel Magal)

## EPILOGUE

The glory of Jerusalem in the first century left a lasting impression on all who walked her streets and entered her temple. Yet, unspeakable tragedy visited the Holy City in A.D. 70 when the Roman army burned the temple and pulled down its walls. The citizens of the city were driven from their ancestral home and forbidden from entering it, except on one day a year—the Day of Atonement. One such visit is remembered in rabbinic lore, and it captures both the horror and the hope engendered at the sight of Jerusalem's devastation.

> It happened that Rabban Gamaliel, Rabbi Elazar ben Azaria, Rabbi Joshua and Rabbi Akiva went up to Jerusalem. When they reached Mount Scopus [overlooking Jerusalem], they tore their garments. When they reached the Temple Mount, they saw a fox emerging from the place of the Holy of Holies. The others started weeping; Rabbi Akiva laughed.
>
> Said they to him: "Why are you laughing?"
>
> Said he to them: "Why are you weeping?"
>
> Said they to him: "A place [so holy] that it is said of it, 'the stranger that approaches it shall die' (Num 1:51), and now foxes traverse it, and we shouldn't weep?"
>
> Said he to them: "That is why I laugh. For it is written, 'And I got reliable witnesses, Uriah the priest and Zechariah the son of Jeberechiah, to attest for me' (Isa 8:2). Now what is the connection between Uriah and Zechariah? Uriah was [in the time of] the First Temple, and Zechariah was [in the time of] the Second Temple! But the Torah makes Zechariah's prophecy dependent upon Uriah's prophecy. With Uriah, it is written: 'There-

fore because of you Zion shall be plowed as a field; Jerusalem shall become a heap of ruins, and the mountain of the house a wooded height' (Mic 3:12). With Zechariah it is written, 'Old men and old women shall again sit in the streets of Jerusalem' (Zech 8:4).

"As long as Uriah's prophecy had not been fulfilled, I feared that Zechariah's prophecy may not be fulfilled either. But now that Uriah's prophecy has been fulfilled, it is certain that Zechariah's prophecy will be fulfilled."

With these words they replied to him: "Akiva, you have consoled us! Akiva, you have consoled us!"

(*b. Mak.* 24b)

It is not Jewish literature alone that speaks of the hope for Jerusalem's future. A sentiment similar to Akiva's prophetic cycle of destruction, repentance and redemption is attributed also to Jesus. Foreseeing the looming disaster, Jesus encouraged his disciples that in that darkest hour they should not lose hope.

But when you see Jerusalem surrounded by armies, then know that its desolation has come near.…For great distress shall be upon the earth and wrath upon this people; they will fall by the edge of the sword, and be led captive among all nations; and Jerusalem will be trodden down by the Gentiles.…Now when these things begin to take place, look up and raise your heads, because your liberation is drawing near. (Luke 21:20, 23–24, 28)

Hope for Jerusalem's future continued into the final book of the New Testament where the city assumed heavenly dimensions. Its redemption embodies the eternal hope of humanity to realize God's salvation and the end of human suffering.

And I saw the holy city, new Jerusalem, coming down out of heaven from God, prepared as a bride adorned for her husband; and I heard a loud voice from the throne saying, "Behold, the dwelling of God is with men. He will dwell with them, and they shall be his people, and God himself will be with them; he will wipe away every tear from their eyes, and death shall be no more, neither shall there be mourning nor crying nor pain any more, for the former things have passed away. (Rev 21:2–4)

## A Prayer for Jerusalem

Pray for the peace of Jerusalem:
May they prosper who love you.
May there be peace be within your walls,
and security within your towers.
For the sake of my relatives and friends
I will say, "Peace be within you."
For the sake of the house of the Lord our God,
I will seek your good.

(Psalms 122:6–9)

# Index

## A



## B

## C

## K



## L



## M

## S



## T

## U



## V



## W



## X



## Y



## Z